Your Rights as a Consumer

Legal Tips for Savvy Purchasing of Goods, Services and Credit

Second Edition

By
Marc R. Lieberman

CAREER PRESS
180 Fifth Avenue
P.O. Box 34
Hawthorne, NJ 07507
1-800-CAREER-1
201-427-0229 (outside U.S.)
FAX: 201-427-2037

YOUR RIGHTS AS A CONSUMER: LEGAL TIPS FOR SAVVY
PURCHASING OF GOODS, SERVICES AND CREDIT
ISBN 1-56414-083-0, $8.95
Cover design by The Gottry Communications Group, Inc.
Series Editor: Richard L. Strohm, Produced by Ronald Adamson, Tucson
Printed in the U.S.A. by Book-mart Press

To order this title by mail, please include price as noted above, $2.50 handling per order, and $1.00 for each book ordered. Send to: Career Press, Inc., 180 Fifth Ave., P.O. Box 34, Hawthorne, NJ 07507.

Or call toll-free 1-800-CAREER-1 (Canada: 201-427-0229) to order using VISA or MasterCard, or for further information on books from Career Press.

Library of Congress Cataloging-in-Publication Data

Lieberman, Marc R., 1956-
    Your rights as a consumer : legal tips for savvy purchasing of goods, services, and credit / by Marc R. Lieberman. -- 2nd ed.
       p.   cm.
   ISBN 1-56414-083-0 : $8.95
    1. Consumer protection--Law and legislation--United States--Popular works. I. Title.
   KF1610.L54   1994
   343.73'071--dc20
   [347.30371]   94-1171
                                         CIP

ACKNOWLEDGEMENTS

This book is dedicated to my grandmothers Rose and Heddy who have enriched my life with their love, chutzpah, and chicken soup. Many thanks to my partners David Dodge and Susan Sendrow, neither of whom makes very good chicken soup, but who have spent countless hours of their valuable time critiquing this manuscript. Thanks to my secretary, Anna Carnahan, who complains she's typed drafts of the manuscript so many times the text intrudes on her dreams. And most of all, thanks to my beautiful wife, Cindy, who says that if I write another book, it better be about divorce.

Marc R. Lieberman

TABLE OF CONTENTS

INTRODUCTION

A "CONSUMER" IS YOU!

Anyone who hires someone to perform a service, or buys something to eat, possess or use, is a "consumer." In other words, a consumer is you!

The law of consumerism is as varied as the goods or services we purchase. The law is further complicated by the fact that the laws of one state often conflict with those of another, and even in circumstances where two states' laws are similar, they may differ from those imposed by the federal government. This book will attempt to make some sense of it all, providing some "bright-line" rules, and some helpful hints, about your rights and obligations as a consumer of goods and services.

One word of caution. The information in this book has been oversimplified, at times, for purposes of clarity. Therefore, while this book will certainly give you a general understanding of your many rights as a consumer, you should not use it as a substitute for the advice of a licensed attorney about a particular situation in which you are involved.

Only after speaking with a qualified attorney can you truly understand your rights in a particular circumstance. The author and publisher urge you to seek such counsel.

CHAPTER ONE:
WHERE YOUR RIGHTS COME FROM

To best understand your rights and obligations as a consumer, an elementary understanding of the "law of contracts" is helpful. Don't panic! The basic law of contracts is easy to understand.

The law of contracts is derived from two sources: "statutes" and the "common law." Statutes are laws enacted by state legislatures or the U.S. Congress. The common law is a body of legal rules established by state or federal courts.

The common law, or judge-made law, is the foundation of the law of contracts, for judges were establishing laws to govern contractual relations hundreds of years before statutes were first enacted for this purpose. Generally, statutes prevail over the common law when there is a conflict between the two. In those instances where no statute applies, but there exists a common law rule governing a situation, the common law rule will control.

> *The law of contracts is derived from two sources: "statutes" and the "common law."*

Suppose a series of court decisions has established the rule that no contract will be enforced unless each party has obtained his mother's written consent. If no statute addresses the issue, the rule established by the court decisions, that is, the common law, will control. However, if a statute is enacted which allows contracts to be enforced without mother approval, the statute will control and the common law rule will be ignored.

How Contracts Are Created

Under the common law, a binding contract is made between two parties as soon as (1) an offer is made by one of the parties; (2) the offer is accepted without major change by the other party; and (3) "consideration" exists for the deal. Consideration exists if each of the parties has provided the other with some benefit. In a typical transaction where the consumer pays a retailer for a product, consideration exists for the exchange since the retailer has benefitted by receipt of the consumer's money and the consumer has benefitted by receipt of the retailer's product.

What You Give Need Not Equal What You Get

Although it seems unfair, the consideration exchanged between the parties does not have to be equal. In most situations, therefore, you have no recourse if you end up paying more for an item than it is actually worth. Thus, you must be a careful shopper. You will be entitled to cancel your purchase, however, if you can show you made the purchase because of the seller's lies or misrepresentations.

Under the common law, , an oral agreement is as binding as a written agreement prepared by lawyers.

Oral Contracts Are Valid

Many people believe that contracts must be in writing and signed by both parties. Under the common law, however, an oral agreement is as binding as a written agreement prepared by lawyers. Obviously, the terms of an agreement are easier to prove when those terms are set forth on paper. For this reason, you should document your agreements whenever possible. Lawyers sometimes joke that people who fail to document their transactions buy more than what they've bargained for—they've bought a dispute, or maybe even a lawsuit as well!

Once a contract is formed, the parties may orally change it, even if their original agreement was in writing and prohibited oral changes. However, a contract's terms cannot be changed by just one of the parties without the other's consent. Such a change is considered a "breach of contract," which is simply one party's failure to do what he promised. Generally, if a party breaches his contractual obligations, the other party will be entitled to all "damages" he suffers.

Damages Are Reasonably Foreseeable Losses

"Damages" are usually the monetary losses suffered because of another's breach of contract. Under the common law, the damages recoverable for another's breach of contract are only those "reasonably foreseeable" as a result of the breach. Thus, a person victimized by another's breach of contract is entitled to recover his out-of-pocket losses, or even the amount of money he would have received if the breaching party had honored the contract. He also may be entitled to cancel the contract and demand the parties be placed in the position each was in before the contract was made. However, the non-breaching party cannot obtain damages the other party could never have anticipated.

"Damages" are usually the monetary losses suffered because of another's breach of contract.

For example, suppose that you pay a courier $25 to deliver papers to an important out-of-town meeting scheduled for 4 o'clock p.m. the following day. While you know that if the papers arrive late, you will be unable to close a million-dollar business deal, this situation is not disclosed to the courier. The papers are not timely delivered and you lose millions of dollars as a result. In these circumstances, you are only entitled to the return of your $25 delivery fee under a breach of contract theory, for the courier could not possibly have known his late delivery would cost you millions of dollars in damages.

An Avalanche of Statutes

The simple rules just described are the basic rules developed by the common law for governing contractual relations. As you can see, the common law rules are fairly straightforward. Our legislators, however, could not leave well enough alone. Over the past 75 years, state legislatures and the U.S. Congress have been busy enacting an avalanche of complicated statutes changing the common law "for the public good." Most of the statutes enacted do protect consumers. Yet, as Mark Twain often said, "No man is safe while Congress is in session," and some of the statutes changing the common law have been enacted to protect industry and limit a consumer's rights and remedies. Much of the remainder of this book will discuss the statutes most impacting our lives as consumers.

Some of the statutes changing the common law have been enacted to protect industry and limit a consumer's rights and remedies.

CHAPTER TWO:
DEALING WITH MERCHANTS

Your Rights Under The UCC

Before the 1950s, the consumer laws of the 50 states differed from one another. Since consumers were unsure of their rights and obligations when purchasing goods out-of-state, they limited such purchases. To promote greater interstate trade, a group of scholars wrote the "Uniform Commercial Code." The Code, or "UCC" for short, is a set of simplified rules governing consumer transactions which the Code's authors urged every state to adopt, thus making the consumer laws throughout America so "uniform" that interstate purchases would no longer be avoided.

Today, the dreams of the UCC's authors have come true, for the UCC has now been adopted, with slight variations, in every American state. The rules in the UCC control most consumer purchases. Therefore, a general familiarity with the UCC's basic provisions will help you understand your rights and obligations in many kinds of everyday transactions.

To promote greater interstate trade, a group of scholars wrote the "Uniform Commercial Code."

Services And Real Estate Are Not Covered

The UCC only applies to sales of "goods" as opposed to services. "Goods" are simply anything that can be easily moved. Since land or homes permanently attached to land cannot be readily moved, they are not goods subject to the UCC. However, minerals, mobile homes, timber and crops are goods since they can be easily removed from the land. Even animals are goods subject to the UCC.

Purchases Of $500 Or More Must Be In Writing

The UCC has changed the common law in many ways. For example, while all oral contracts are enforceable at common law, under the UCC, you can enforce a contract for the purchase of goods priced at $500 or more only if it is in writing and signed by the other party or his agent.

There are three exceptions to the writing requirement. First, no writing is required if the goods ordered were to be specially made for the buyer, cannot be sold to the seller's other customers, and the seller has taken significant steps to manufacture or obtain the goods. Second, no writing is required if the party against whom enforcement of the contract is sought admits the existence of the contract. Third, no writing is required if the goods ordered have been accepted. Written contracts do not have to be in any particular form.

Acceptances Varying An Offer's Terms

The UCC also has changed the common law rule that no contract exists if an "acceptance" of an offer varies the offer's terms. Under the UCC, an acceptance that varies the terms of the offer creates a binding agreement based on the original offer's terms. The terms of the acceptance that are different from those stated in the offer are considered proposed additions to the contract, which the original offeror can accept or reject.

Prohibitions Against Oral Changes

The UCC has even changed the common law rule that contracts can be orally changed, despite written prohibitions to the contrary. The

UCC says that provisions in a written contract prohibiting oral changes will be enforced. However, such prohibitions cannot be enforced against a consumer unless the consumer specifically agrees to this in a separate writing.

If a contract, as orally changed, still involves the sale of an item valued at $500 or more, the changed contract will not be enforced unless it too is in writing, unless one or more of the exceptions to the writing requirement earlier discussed apply.

Relief From The Awful Bargain

At common law, consumers who got what they paid for but paid too much had little recourse. Under the UCC, however, consumers can nullify purchases that are shockingly unfair, and resulting from unfair pressure. Such purchases are called "unconscionable." That is, they "shock the conscience." Mere parts of a contract can be held unenforceable as unconscionable. Courts have found contracts unconscionable in situations where the seller has charged the buyer a dramatically excessive price and/or unduly limited the buyer's remedies or unduly increased his own. The classic unconscionable purchase is where a door-to-door salesman convinces an unsophisticated or elderly consumer to buy an ordinary product for three times or more than its true retail value.

Consumers can nullify purchases that are shockingly unfair, and which result from unfair pressure.

While unconscionability is a useful tool for setting aside horribly bad bargains, the courts are hesitant to find contracts unconscionable except in the most egregious of cases. Therefore, your most useful weapon for protecting yourself from bad bargains is simply to avoid them.

"Reasonable" Is The Name Of The Game

The overriding theme of the UCC is "reasonableness." The UCC is riddled with provisions requiring the parties to act reasonably toward one another. For example, the UCC says that if no time for shipment or delivery of goods is specified, shipment or delivery shall be within a "reasonable time." Likewise, if a contract is made for the purchase of goods but the price of the goods remains unsettled, the price is to be a "reasonable" one. Similarly, where a contract provides for monthly shipments of goods but is indefinite in duration, the contract will be valid for a "reasonable" period, or until terminated by either party. The UCC even says each party to a contract must act in good faith and in a "reasonable" manner.

The UCC does not define "reasonable." Many judges have defined "reasonable" to mean what an average responsible person would consider appropriate in the circumstances. The term is certainly not capable of exact definition.

A famous judge once commented that while he could not define what was obscene, he "knew it when he saw it." In much the same way, you will know, instinctively, whether you are being treated in a reasonable fashion. If you suspect you are not, it is possible the seller has violated one of the Code's many provisions imposing reasonable conduct and terms, thus giving you some recourse against the seller.

When Credit Periods Run

One of the most important concessions to industry contained in the UCC is the rule regarding when credit periods run. Unless otherwise agreed, if goods are to be shipped to you on credit, the credit period — that is, the date you begin to be charged interest on your purchase, starts the moment goods are shipped to you. This means you may pay far more on credit purchases of goods taking considerable periods to ship, such as items you can obtain only by cargo vessel. To avoid interest charges on items with long transit periods, simply ask the seller to delay charging interest until you actually receive the goods. The seller is likely to agree to this if you are purchasing a "big ticket" item. If the seller will not agree to delay the beginning of interest until delivery, purchase the item with a credit card allowing you a 30-day grace period (see page 59) before interest begins to be charged against your purchase.

The Four Warranties

Arguably, the most important provisions of the UCC are the Code's "warranty" provisions. The UCC allows or imposes four kinds of warranties: "express" warranties, and warranties of "fitness," "merchantability," and "title." Each of these is discussed below.

Express Warranties

Any statement of fact, or promise, made by a seller relating to goods he has sold you creates an "express warranty," or guarantee by the seller, that the goods will conform with his statement or promise. In other words, if a seller tells you that a watch is waterproof to get you to purchase it, such a statement, if untrue, will entitle you to obtain damages against the seller for breach of an "express warranty."

Any statement of fact, or promise, made by a seller relating to goods he has sold you creates an "express warranty."

9

The seller need not use formal words like, "I warrant" or "I guarantee" to create an express warranty. And the seller does not have to intend to make an express warranty. So long as a statement made by a seller is relied on by the purchaser in forming his decision to buy goods, the seller is considered to have "expressly warranted," or guaranteed, that the goods conform with his statement.

Suppose a seller shows you a sample or model of what he says the goods will look or act like. That creates an express warranty that the goods will conform to the model or sample, so long as your decision to purchase the goods was based on the characteristics of the model or sample.

Statements Of Opinion And Value Are Not Warrantable

There are two notable exceptions to the rules regarding creation of express warranties. First, a seller's statement about the value of goods does not create a warranty that the goods are truly worth the value represented. Thus, if a salesman tells you a boat is worth $15,000, or could fetch that amount upon resale, he is not considered to have warranted that the boat is worth what he said. Because you cannot rely on a seller's statement about the value of goods, you should always confirm the worth of the goods from independent sources.

A second exception to the general rule regarding creation of express warranties is that a seller's statements of opinion about goods, as opposed to statements of fact, do not create an express warranty that the goods conform with his expressed opinions. For example, if an antique dealer tells you, "This vase is 100 years old," the dealer will be considered to have warranted that the age of the vase is as he said. In contrast, if the dealer merely says, "This vase could be 100 years old," this statement of opinion, as opposed to fact, will not be considered a warranty.

Knowing they cannot be held accountable for statements of opinion, many unscrupulous sellers dole out opinions by the bucketful, while minimizing statements of fact. Consumers attuned to the difference between statements of fact and opinion will undoubtedly make more informed purchase decisions.

Knowing they cannot be held accountable for statements of opinion, many unscrupulous sellers dole out opinions by the bucketful.

The Implied Warranties Of Title, Merchantability And Fitness

A second kind of warranty recognized by the UCC is the "Implied Warranty." An "implied" warranty is simply a warranty imposed by law rather than expressly stated by the seller. An implied warranty will exist unless it is properly excluded, as we will discuss later. There are three types of implied warranties. The first of these, the implied warranty of title, is explained below.

The Implied Warranty Of Title

When someone has "title " to goods, he holds the goods free of the claims of all other people. The UCC says that when you buy goods from a seller regularly dealing in goods of that kind, that seller implicitly "warrants," or, guarantees you, that no one else can claim he owns the goods you purchased. The "warranty of title" can be excluded only if the seller specifically disclaims it before your purchase or there exists circumstances giving the buyer reason to know the seller lacks sufficient right to transfer title to the goods.

The classic case of a buyer not being able to rely on the warranty of title is where he buys an item at a price so outrageously low that he suspects the item may be stolen. If his suspicions turn out to be well-founded, and his "steal" turns out to have been stolen, upon recovery of the item by the police, the buyer has no recourse against the seller who sold him the item. The circumstances of the purchase made it reasonably clear that the buyer was purchasing "hot" goods whose title the seller had no right to convey.

The Implied Warranty Of Merchantability

Another implied warranty imposed by the UCC is the "implied warranty of merchantability." Generally, the implied warranty of merchantability is a guarantee implicitly made by all sellers that the goods they sell (1) are non-objectionable to other sellers of like merchandise; (2) are of at least fair to average quality; (3) are suitable for the purpose for which such goods are sold; (4) are adequately packaged and labeled; and (5) conform to the statements made on their containers or labels. Goods which do not satisfy each of the five elements are not "merchantable," and a buyer has various remedies available to address the situation.

The implied warranty of merchantability only applies to sales of goods by sellers who regularly sell such goods.

The implied warranty of merchantability only applies to sales of goods by sellers who regularly sell such goods. Thus, someone who is not a car dealer can sell his car without fear that he has implicitly warranted the car to be "merchantable."

Suppose, on a visit to a local drug store, you buy some brand name permanent wave solution to curl your hair. If the solution curls your hair to a fair degree, it is "merchantable." If through no fault of your own the solution turns your hair green, it is not merchantable, for the solution is certainly not suitable for the purpose for which it was sold.

The Implied Warranty Of Fitness

The UCC imposes a third implied warranty in addition to those of "title" and "merchantability." This third implied warranty is that of "fitness for a particular purpose," or "fitness" for short. The implied warranty of fitness applies where the seller has reason to know, at the time of your purchase, the purpose for which you intend to use his product. If the seller also knows, at the time of purchase, that you are relying on his judgment and expertise to furnish you with a product suitable for your purpose, he implicitly warrants that the goods he provides you are fit or useful for that purpose.

The implied warranty of fitness applies where the seller has reason to know the purpose for which you intend to use his product.

Suppose you know nothing about computers but wish to buy one your children can use to learn a foreign language. If, after telling this to a computer salesman, he sells you a computer incapable of being operated by youngsters or teaching them a foreign language, the salesman has breached his warranty of fitness.

Like all implied warranties, the warranty of fitness can be excluded or changed, but only in accordance with the rules set forth below.

How Warranties Can Be Excluded Or Changed

All implied warranties, other than "title," are excluded if the goods are purchased "as is."

As you might expect, all implied warranties, other than "title," are excluded if the goods are purchased "as is," "with all faults," or by other terms which are commonly understood as meaning no implied warranties are intended. Before purchasing the goods, if you have examined them as much as you liked, or refused to examine them, no implied warranties exist with regard to defects which your examination should have revealed!

If goods are not sold "as is" or with similar language, and no defects would be apparent upon inspection, the implied warranty of "merchantability" can be excluded or changed only if the exclusion or change specifically mentions "merchantability" and, if in writing, is "conspicuous." In other words, the implied warranty of merchantability can be orally excluded or changed, but only if the seller specifically tells you so; and if the sale is documented in writing, any exclusion or change in the warranty must be in bold-faced type and specifically reference "merchantability."

Excluding or changing the implied warranty of fitness is even tougher. Such exclusions must be in writing and be conspicuous. The seller does not have to mention the word "fitness," though, to exclude the warranty of fitness. A mere written statement to the effect, "There are no warranties other than described herein," or similar statement, is sufficient to exclude the implied warranty of fitness.

The seller can exclude or change the implied warranty of title only if he orally or in writing excludes or changes it, or, as earlier mentioned, the buyer has reason to know the seller does not warrant title. Unlike exclusions or changes to warranties of merchantability and fitness, exclusions or changes to warranties of title are rare. Sellers who will not guarantee their goods as being free of the claims of other persons are likely to have few, if any, customers.

One caveat. The federal government has enacted statutes severely limiting a seller's right to exclude or change implied warranties when a written warranty or service agreement is made. These federal statutes are discussed in Chapter 5.

Who Can Rely On Warranties

Ordinarily, unless otherwise agreed, or unless the seller knows the goods are being purchased for use by another identified person, only the buyer can enforce an express or implied warranty. However, the UCC provides that both express and implied warranties will extend to anyone in the buyer's family or household, including his guests, if any of these people become injured by the goods and if it is reasonable to expect that those injured might use, consume or otherwise be affected by the goods.

The UCC provides that both express and implied warranties will extend to anyone in the buyer's family or household.

The case of the poison pizza is a good example of this rule. If your local pizza parlor sells you a pizza with spoiled sausage, and your family or guests eat the pizza and become ill, those injured could sue the pizza parlor, even though they did not purchase the pizza directly.

The Rules For Performance

After you contract to purchase an item, what are your rights concerning performance of the contract? To a great extent, the contract terms determine your rights. If the contract is silent on particular issues, the UCC provides many rules to fill in the gaps. The most important of these rules are set forth below.

No Pay, No Play

Unless otherwise agreed, you have no duty to pay for goods unless the seller tenders them, that is, provides them to you. Conversely, and unless otherwise agreed, you have no right to keep goods sold you if you do not pay for them. In other words, if your check for goods "bounces" and is returned unpaid for insufficient funds, you have no right to keep the goods.

Your Right To Inspect

After your inspection, if you reject the goods as unsuitable, the seller must pay your inspection costs.

Unless otherwise agreed, or unless goods are purchased "C.O.D.," that is, Cash On Delivery, you have the right to inspect goods before paying for them. You must bear the cost of any inspection, unless you reject the goods because they are unsuitable. After your inspection, if you reject the goods as unsuitable, the seller must pay your inspection costs.

If a seller tenders goods which, upon inspection, you find unsuitable, the seller may substitute suitable goods if his time for performing his end of the bargain has not expired.

Shipment

How goods will be delivered to you is an important element of any purchase where shipment is necessary. All too often, consumers pay little attention to shipment details, and this may cost them dearly.

In most "typical" consumer transactions where goods are to be delivered, they are shipped by familiar means, such as the mail or parcel post. In circumstances where the goods involved are so large or heavy they cannot be shipped by familiar means, the seller may ship them to you FOB, FAS, CIF, C.F. or C&F. What do those terms mean?

FOB means "free on board." It usually refers to shipments by train or truck. FAS means "free alongside." It means the same thing as FOB, except FAS usually refers to shipments by boat. If goods are shipped to you "FOB place of shipment" or "FAS place of shipment," that means the seller will pay only the cost of getting the goods to the carrier that is supposed to deliver them to you. In other words, you, the buyer, will have to pay all costs of shipment from the place where the carrier receives the goods from the seller! In contrast, if goods are shipped to you "FOB place of destination," or "FAS place of destination," the seller must pay all costs of delivering the goods to you. Obviously, you should insist all goods be shipped to you FOB or FAS "place of destination."

FOB or FAS "place of destination" contracts are especially advantageous to the buyer because a seller has no responsibility for damage to the goods once he has delivered them, in good condition, to a carrier under an FOB or FAS "place of shipment" type contract. If the contract is FOB or FAS "place of destination," however, the seller will bear the cost of any damage to the goods until they are actually delivered to the buyer.

Suppose you live in Chicago and buy a car which is to be shipped to you from San Francisco under "FOB place of shipment" terms. After the seller places the car with a trucking firm in San Francisco, the car is later destroyed in a traffic accident while it is enroute to be delivered to you. In these circumstances, the seller is not responsible for the car's destruction and you must pay him the full purchase price! However, if the sale was "FOB place of destination," the seller would be responsible for providing you with a substitute car or, if that was not feasible, returning the purchase price.

"CIF" contracts are those where the price of the goods you have bought includes the cost of the goods as well as the insurance and freight charges required to ship them to you. A "C.F." or "C&F" purchase means the same thing, except insurance for the shipment is not included.

> *Insist that goods shipped to you are sent CIF, or at the very least, FOB or FAS "place of destination."*

Insist that goods shipped to you are sent CIF, or at the very least, FOB or FAS "place of destination." Under such arrangements, delivery of the goods to you is guaranteed. Moreover, the cost of shipment is built into the purchase price, and you will not be surprised, upon delivery, with a shipping bill much larger than you had reason to expect.

Your Right To Reject Goods

If the goods delivered do not conform to the terms of sale, you are entitled to accept them, reject them, or accept any part and reject the rest.

Your rejection of the goods must be within a "reasonable" time after the delivery, and the rejection is ineffective unless you promptly tell the seller of your rejection. After you reject goods, you cannot use them. And if you have taken possession of the goods, you also must care for them in a "reasonable" manner until the seller has a chance to take them back. If the seller fails to reclaim the goods within a "reasonable" time after you reject them, you may (1) ship the goods back to the seller at the seller's cost; (2) store them for the seller at the seller's cost; or (3) sell them to third persons, for the seller's benefit. If you sell the goods, the seller is entitled to all sale proceeds, but you are entitled to reimbursement from the seller, out of the sale proceeds, of all "reasonable" expenses of caring for and selling the goods.

Note that when you reject goods, you should always specify your reasons for the rejection. If you do not, and the rejection results from a defect which is apparent upon reasonable inspection and could have been cured by the seller if he had known of it, your rejection is invalid!

Acceptance Of Goods

After you have a "reasonable" opportunity to inspect the goods, if you then inform the seller, by words or deeds, that the goods are suitable or that you will keep them even if they are not suitable, you will be deemed to have "accepted" the goods. Your "acceptance" is significant because acceptance triggers your duty to pay for the goods and, in most instances, prevents you from rejecting them. Your acceptance can be revoked, however, if you later discover hidden defects or a breach of warranty.

Your "acceptance" is significant because acceptance triggers your duty to pay for the goods.

Before you accept goods, the seller must establish that the goods are suitable. Once you accept goods, however, the burden is on you to establish their unsuitability. Because of this, you should withhold your acceptance until you are convinced the goods are suitable in every respect.

After you accept goods, if you discover the goods are defective or otherwise unsuitable, and you wish to revoke your acceptance, you must notify the seller within a "reasonable time." If you do not, you may be denied any recourse against the seller.

Remedies For The Seller's Breach

If a seller fails to deliver goods as promised, or indicates he will not honor his bargain, or if you justifiably reject goods or rightfully revoke your acceptance of them, the UCC allows you several remedies. In all cases, you may cancel your contract and demand your money back. In addition, you can demand the difference between what you originally agreed to pay the seller and what it would reasonably cost you to buy similar goods elsewhere. Moreover, you can "cover," which means you can actually purchase substitute goods. In the latter two cases, you also would be entitled to demand your "incidental" and "consequential" damages.

"Incidental"
damages are
any reasonable
expense caused
by the seller's
delay or breach
of contract.

Incidental Damages

"Incidental" damages are any reasonable expense caused by the seller's delay or breach of contract. For example, if you "cover" and purchase substitute goods, your incidental damages might include any expenses or commissions you pay to obtain the substitute goods. Likewise, incidental damages recoverable as a result of your rejection of unsuitable goods might include your reasonable expenses to inspect, transport, store or otherwise care for the rejected goods.

Consequential Damages

Generally, "consequential" damages are reasonably foreseeable losses suffered as a result of the seller's breach and which could not reasonably be prevented. Examples of consequential losses are any personal injuries or property damage resulting from a breach of warranty.

Forced Delivery

If the seller fails or refuses to deliver goods, and you cannot obtain appropriate substitutes, you may also demand that the seller deliver the goods upon your payment of the full purchase price. Courts are especially likely to force a seller to deliver goods if those goods are unique and cannot be produced elsewhere.

Damages For Breach Of Warranty

The measure of damages for any breach of warranty is the difference between the actual value of the goods and what their value would have been if no breach of warranty had occurred. You also can obtain any incidental or consequential damages resulting from a breach of warranty.

Deduction Of Damages From Price

In all cases where the seller has breached his contract and you have suffered damages as a result, you are entitled to deduct all or part of your damages from any part of the purchase price still due under your contract. You must, however, notify the seller of your intentions.

Remedies For The Buyer's Breach

If the buyer wrongfully rejects or revokes his acceptance of goods, fails to pay or otherwise fails to honor his part of the bargain, the seller can withhold delivery, stop delivery of the goods if they are in transit, and/or cancel the contract. The seller can even resell the goods to someone else and demand that the buyer reimburse him for any losses he's suffered due to the resale. However, such a demand will not be lawful unless the seller notifies the buyer that he will resell the goods.

If the buyer wrongfully rejects or revokes his acceptance of goods, the seller can cancel the contract.

If the buyer unjustifiably rejects or revokes his acceptance of goods and returns them to the seller, the seller can demand the purchaser pay him the difference between what he actually is able to resell the goods for and what the buyer was supposed to pay him, together with any "incidental" damages suffered. And if that is not enough to put the seller in the position he would have been in had the buyer honored his bargain, the seller will be entitled to demand that the buyer pay him all profit, including reasonable overhead, the seller would have made, together with any incidental damages.

The seller can always sue a buyer for the price of goods accepted but not paid for. If a buyer wrongfully refuses to accept goods, however, the seller can sue the buyer for the purchase price only if he is unable to resell the goods at a reasonable price.

Liquidation Of Damages

Contracts for the sale of goods often contain "liquidated damage" provisions. A "liquidated" sum is an exact sum, whereas an "unliquidated" sum is undetermined. Liquidated damage provisions are terms specifying the exact amount of damage either party will be deemed to have suffered as a result of the other's breach. By specifying the exact amount of damages payable upon breach, the parties are relieved of the burden of establishing the amount of their actual damages and the parties can easily know their rights and liabilities.

Unfortunately, liquidated damage provisions in many sale contracts are one-sided and unfair. For example, many liquidated damage provisions only specify the damages payable by the buyer to the seller upon the buyer's breach of contract, and not vice-versa. Further, the liquidated damages to be paid by the buyer often are much larger than the actual harm that would result from the buyer's breach of contract. While the UCC does not necessarily prohibit one-sided liquidated damage provisions, it does not allow unreasonably large liquidated damages. Unreasonably large liquidated damages far exceed the actual damages that would most likely occur.

Limitation Of Damages

In general, the parties may provide for remedies in addition to or different from those specified in the UCC. A sale contract can limit the remedies otherwise available to buyers under the UCC. However, a contract severely restricting the buyer's remedies may be held unenforceable as unconscionable. Limiting the buyer's right to demand damages for personal injuries is almost always prohibited as unconscionable.

The Statute Of Limitations

Under the common law, there were few, if any time limits to sue someone for a breach of contract. The UCC imposes specific time limits, however, for bringing a lawsuit for breach of contract. These time limits are called "Statutes of Limitation." Generally, the statute of limitation for bringing suit under the UCC is four years. Thus, an action for breach of any contract involving goods must be filed within four years of the breach of contract, regardless of when the wronged party learned of the breach. The UCC treats breaches of warranty as occurring when goods are "tendered," that is, placed at the buyer's disposal. The parties may agree to reduce the limitation period, that is, the time limit to bring suit, to not less than one year. The parties cannot extend the limitations period to more than four years.

Generally, the statute of limitation for bringing suit under the UCC is four years.

An "auction" is a public gathering where goods are individually presented for sale and the person making the highest offer for the goods can purchase them. At auctions, offers are called "bids." The UCC controls your rights at auction so long as the auction involves the sale of goods.

Auctions are not conducted by the owner/seller of an item, but instead, by an independent third party called an "auctioneer." The auctioneer is usually paid a small percentage of the auction's receipts, although some auctioneers charge an hourly rate, or even a set fee, for their services.

> *The UCC controls your rights at auction so long as the auction involves the sale of goods.*

In the typical auction, you are given a short period before the bidding begins to examine the items offered for sale. Thereafter, the auctioneer will separately present each item for sale, inviting bids from those attending. Generally, bids are made orally or by hand signal, and usually progress upward from a base figure established by the auctioneer. The auctioneer will continue to invite increasingly higher bids until no bid higher than that previously made is received from the audience. The auctioneer will then signal the bidding to be "complete" by announcing the item bid upon as "sold" and/or rapping a hammer or gavel.

In most cases, items sold at auction are purchased "as is," without any warranties other than that of title. However, nothing prevents auctioneers or the owners of items auctioned from expressly or impliedly warranting goods, and if such warranties are made, or not properly excluded, the auctioneer and/or the former owner of the items will be liable.

Auctions With Or Without "Reserve"

Generally, there are two kinds of auctions — "with reserve" and "without reserve." In auctions "without reserve," an item cannot be withdrawn as available for sale once the auctioneer calls for bids, unless no bids are even made on the item. In auctions "with reserve," the auctioneer may withdraw an item offered anytime up to the moment he announces the sale of that item to be complete. Unless otherwise indicated all auctions are "with reserve."

Auctions "with reserve" are designed to ensure that the highest price possible is received for an auctioned item. If the auctioneer (who is usually receiving a "piece of the action") believes the bids received are too low, he can withdraw the item from bidding and offer it at another time.

An auctioneer is strictly prohibited from knowingly receiving a bid on behalf of the owner/seller of auctioned goods.

Bogus Bidders

To prevent an owner/seller of auctioned goods from artificially inflating the price bid for his goods, an auctioneer is strictly prohibited from knowingly receiving a bid on behalf of the owner/seller of auctioned goods. If the auctioneer knowingly receives a bid from the owner of an auctioned item, or the owner makes such a bid, and notice has not been given that this is allowed, the buyer is entitled to cancel his purchase or take the item not for the price he bid but instead, the price of the last good faith bid.

Professional auctioneers rarely accept bids from persons they know or even suspect to be the owner of auctioned goods, for an auctioneer's most valuable asset is his professional independence and integrity. Once an auction eer's reputation is sullied by news he has colluded with a seller to "rig" an auction, he is unlikely to work again. Indeed, many states consider rigging an auction a crime.

While the vast majority of auctioneers are scrupulously honest, many auctions are "rigged" anyway because owners often hire persons not known to be affiliated with them to bid up the price of the owners' goods at auction. These practices are difficult to stop. Your best defense is simply to establish in your own mind the true value of an item and not bid more than that no matter how the bidding progresses. Remember, because owners can so easily rig an auction by having their secret agents bid up the price of their goods, the fact that an item is receiving bids far in excess of what you thought it was worth is not necessarily an indication of the item's true value.

Bid Procedure

Auctioneers usually invite bids in an orderly fashion, waiting to the last possible moment before declaring a bid complete. Occasionally, a bid will occur while the auctioneer's hammer is falling to accept a prior bid. In such a circumstance, the auctioneer is authorized to either reopen the bidding or instead, declare the goods sold under the bid on which his hammer was falling.

Contrary to popular belief, you can retract or withdraw your bid.

Contrary to popular belief, you can retract or withdraw your bid, so long as you do so orally or by any reasonably understandable signal before the auctioneer announces completion of the sale. If a bid is withdrawn, this does not revive the previous bid.

Suppose that, after you bid $50 for a lamp, another bidder offers $75 but immediately withdraws his bid. Your $50 bid will not be automatically revived. Instead, you will have to make another bid to have a chance at buying the lamp.

All of the rules in the UCC and explained in Chapter Two apply at merchandise auctions unless the auctioneer announces different rules will apply. Most auctioneers or their firms called "auction houses," require successful bidders to pay cash or its equivalent, and arrangements for delivery are usually the buyer's responsibility. The rules of many auction houses provide that if the buyer fails to pay for goods within a designated period, typically 24 hours, the auction house may cancel the sale, re-offer the goods for auction or, if possible, offer them to the next highest bidder.

Generally, all of the rules in the UCC and explained in Chapter Two apply at merchandise auctions.

CHAPTER FOUR:
CONSUMER FRAUD LAWS

Your Recourse For Rip-Off

As famous circus promoter P. T. Barnum remarked well before the turn of the 20th century, "There's a sucker born every minute." Unfortunately, each of us has been suckered from time to time by unscrupulous salespersons. Fortunately, since Mr. Barnum's time, the U.S. Congress and each of the state legislatures have enacted many statutes to prevent and remedy fraudulent or deceptive sales practices. Often, these statutes provide severe penalties for violators.

In this chapter, we first will examine some federal and state statutes broadly prohibiting "unfair or deceptive" sales practices. We next will examine some federal and state statutes which are designed to protect consumers in specific kinds of transactions where they often have been victimized.

The Federal Trade Commission

The Federal Trade Commission, or "FTC", is a federal agency created by the U.S. Congress in the early 1900's to prevent unfair or deceptive sales practices. Congress has enacted federal statutes broadly prohibiting "false advertisements," "unfair methods of competition," and "unfair or deceptive acts or practices," and the FTC can prosecute violations of these statutes, as well as issue orders to prevent violations.

> *Congress has enacted federal statutes broadly prohibiting "false advertisements."*

False Advertisements

Federal statutes define "false advertisements" as those which are misleading in a significant way. An ad can be considered misleading not only by what it says but what it fails to say. For example, an ad by a publishing company promising authors a large royalty on any book submitted for publication was considered false since the ad failed to mention each author would have to pay most publishing costs! Similarly, an ad promising that a product was "guaranteed for life" was branded false because it did not explain that buyers had to purchase a lifetime service agreement before any lifetime guarantee would apply.

It is unlawful for an advertiser to quote a small part of a newspaper or magazine article discussing his product if the quote creates an impression different from that the article as a whole sought to convey. And advertisers using illustrations must ensure these illustrations do not mislead the public. Thus, a print ad promoting the sale of mink coats for $7500 or less is unlawful if it pictures a model wearing a $50,000 coat. Likewise, television ads showing certain passenger cars as being capable of withstanding spectacularly crushing impacts are unlawful if they fail to disclose that the cars pictured, unlike those available for sale, have been specially modified.

Mislabelling

The federal statutes prohibiting unfair methods of competition and deceptive acts also prohibit mislabelling of products. In fact, if a label is not truthful in nearly every respect, the label will be considered unlawful.

The FTC is anxious to prosecute distribution of mislabelled merchandise. In one case, the

FTC prohibited a distributor from selling underwear labeled "natural wool" simply because the underwear was not 100% wool, although it was mostly wool.

Misleading Discount, Rebate, Promotion Or Sale Offers

False or misleading discount, sale and rebate offers are also prohibited as unfair and deceptive practices. A seller who artificially inflates the retail price of his goods so that his "sale," discount or rebate promotion appears more attractive than it really is has committed an unfair and deceptive practice in violation of federal law. A seller who misleadingly uses test results to promote sales of his goods has violated the law as well.

Remedies For Deceptive Acts

Any misrepresentation by a seller to promote the sale of goods conceivably violates the federal statutes prohibiting unfair or deceptive acts. However, to obtain relief for misleading advertising or deceptive sales practices under the federal law, you cannot sue the seller. Instead, your only recourse under the federal statutes is to report the seller to the FTC. If the FTC believes the seller's conduct to be unlawful, it can order the seller to remedy his misconduct and cease any further unlawful activities. If the seller fails to comply with the FTC's orders, he can be assessed a penalty of up to $10,000 for each violation of the orders.

Naturally, sellers fear FTC scrutiny. Thus, if you have been victimized by unfair or deceptive practices of a seller, you might convince the seller to remedy the situation simply by informing him you

False or misleading discount sale and rebate offers are also prohibited as unfair and deceptive practices.

will seek FTC intervention if relief from the seller is not forthcoming. If the seller nevertheless ignores your demands, you should write or telephone the FTC care of The Director, Bureau of Consumer Protection, Federal Trade Commission, Washington, D.C. 20580, (202) 523-3598.

State Consumer Fraud Acts

The state statutes sometimes are far more useful than their federal counterparts for combatting consumer fraud.

Most state legislatures have enacted numerous statutes aimed at preventing and remedying consumer fraud. The state statutes sometimes are far more useful than their federal counterparts for combatting consumer fraud, first because they often permit consumers to sue for their violation, and second, because they sometimes are directed at conduct which the federal statutes do not expressly address.

General Prohibitions Against Deceptive Ads Or Practices

Inspired by the federal acts prohibiting unfair or deceptive sales practices or advertising, most states have made it unlawful for a business to intentionally use any misleading act or practice, or to conceal important facts, in connection with the sale or advertisement of merchandise. State attorneys general usually can prosecute violations of these laws. Generally, the attorneys general are allowed to seek court orders both prohibiting deceptive practices as well as restoring to consumers any monies they have lost as a result of such practices. The attorneys general even can seek court orders prohibiting violators from engaging in further business.

Like the federal consumer fraud statutes, many state consumer fraud acts provide for a fine of up to $10,000 per violation. Unlike the federal statutes, however, consumers themselves can usually sue for violation of the state consumer fraud statutes. This is an important remedy since state attorneys general are often so overburdened and understaffed that they are reluctant to take action on anything but the most flagrant cases.

If you believe you have been victimized by a deceptive advertisement or sales practice, and you can get no relief from the seller, contact the office of your state attorney general and request a consumer fraud complaint form, which in most instances, you will be required to fill out and return by mail. The attorney general usually will forward a copy of your complaint to the seller and request his response. If the attorney general is not satisfied with the seller's response, an investigation and possible prosecution of the seller may begin. Because lawsuits are often expensive, it is always best to seek relief by way of the FTC and your local attorney general's office before seeking relief on your own in the courts.

Because lawsuits are often expensive, it is always best to seek relief by way of the FTC and your local attorney general's office.

Telephone Solicitations

An increasing number of states are enacting statutes severely restricting salesmen from selling you goods by telephone. Typically, these laws require telephone solicitors to register with the state and post a sizable bond (see page 79) with the state treasurer. The bond may be used to satisfy the claims of persons victimized by a telephone solicitor's misconduct.

Generally, telephone solicitation statutes require telephone solicitors to make various disclosures in connection with any sale of merchandise where some gift, bonus, prize or award is promised as an incentive for the purchase. Usually, the solicitor is required to disclose his complete street address and the seller's name. The solicitor also is required to inform prospective buyers that they have until midnight of the third business day after they receive the goods or "prize," whichever is later, to cancel the sale. If the buyer is not advised, both orally and in writing, of the name, telephone number and complete address of the seller, orally advised of his three-day right of cancellation, and mailed written notice of his right to cancel within 21 days of his receipt of the merchandise or "prize," whichever is later, the sale is invalid. Usually, the written notice of cancellation will be in this form:

Prospective buyers have until midnight of the third business day after they receive the goods or "prize," whichever is later, to cancel the sale.

NOTICE OF CANCELLATION

1. You may cancel this order without any penalty or obligation within three business days from the delivery of the merchandise or premium (gift, bonus, prize or award), whichever is later.

2. If you cancel, any payments made by you will be returned within ten days after receipt by the seller of your notice of cancellation.

3. To cancel this transaction, mail or deliver a signed and dated copy of your cancellation notice or send a telegram to (name of seller) at (seller's address).

4. If you cancel, any merchandise or premium delivered to you must be returned at our expense to (name of seller) at (seller's address).

State attorneys general can prosecute violations of telephone solicitation acts, and many states consider violations of such acts to be felonies. Most telephone solicitation acts also allow consumers to sue for violation of these acts. Consumers victimized by salesmen violating telephone solicitation laws usually can recover all damages resulting from the violation.

Home Solicitations

The FTC and all states except New Mexico have enacted laws limiting a seller's rights in connection with sales of goods at buyers' homes. These laws, often called "Home Solicitation Acts," were originally intended to prevent salesmen from fleecing non-English speaking immigrants by having them sign burdensome sale contracts whose terms were a far cry from what was orally promised them.

You do not have to be an immigrant to take advantage of the Home Solicitation Acts. The Acts generally apply whenever a salesman visits your home uninvited and sells you goods worth $25 or more. Under such circumstances, the sale will not be effective unless (1) a written agreement of it is made; (2) the agreement lists the name and address of the seller and is signed and dated by the buyer; (3) the agreement is in the same language as that used by the salesman in his oral sales pitch; and (4) the agreement states:

The Home Solicitation Acts generally apply whenever a salesman visits your home uninvited and sells you goods worth $25 or more.

YOU, THE BUYER, MAY CANCEL THIS TRANSACTION AT ANY TIME PRIOR TO MIDNIGHT OF THE THIRD BUSINESS DAY AFTER THE DATE OF THIS TRANSACTION. SEE THE ATTACHED NOTICE OF CANCELLATION FORM FOR THE EXPLANATION OF THIS RIGHT.

Two copies of the following form, in the same language as that used in the seller's oral presentation, also must be completed and given the buyer:

NOTICE OF CANCELLATION
[date of transaction]

You may cancel this transaction, without any penalty or obligation, within three business days from the above date.

If you cancel, any property traded in, any payments made by you under the contract or sale and any negotiable instrument executed by you will be returned within ten business days following receipt by the seller of your cancellation notice and any security interests arising out of the transaction will be canceled.

If you cancel, you must make available to the seller at your residence in substantially as good condition as when received, any goods delivered to you under this contract or sale; or you may, if you wish, comply with the instructions of the seller regarding the return shipment of the goods at the seller's expense and risk.

If you do make the goods available to the seller and the seller does not pick them up within twenty days of the date of your notice of cancellation, you may return or dispose of the goods without any further obligation. If you fail to make the goods available to the seller, or if you agree to return the goods to the seller and fail to do so, then you remain liable for performance of all obligations under the contract.

To cancel this transaction, mail or deliver a signed and dated copy of this cancellation notice or any other written notice, or send a telegram, to [name of seller], at [address of seller's place of business] not later than midnight of [date].

I hereby cancel this transaction.

[Date]

_____

Buyer's signature

As the above cancellation notice states, a buyer can cancel any home solicitation sale until midnight of the third "business day" after the day on which the buyer signs the sales contract. The seller must orally inform the buyer of his three-day right to cancel when the contract is made. A "business day" is any day other than a Sunday or federal holiday. Simply placing notice of cancellation in the mail within the three-day period following a sale effectively cancels the sale — the seller need not actually receive the notice within the three-day period.

If a buyer properly cancels a home solicitation contract, the seller has to return the buyer's down payment and any promissory note made by the buyer in connection with the sale within 10 days. If the buyer traded in goods as part of his down payment, the seller must return these

A buyer may cancel any home solicitation sale until midnight of the third "business day."

37

goods in the condition they were in when received. Some state Home Solicitation Acts provide that if the seller fails to return the goods traded, the seller will be liable to the buyer for the trade-in value assigned to the traded goods in the sales contract. The buyer can keep the seller's goods until the seller complies with all of his obligations.

Within 20 days after a buyer cancels a home solicitation sale, the buyer must allow the seller to pick up the goods at the buyer's home. Within ten days of the buyer notifying the seller he intends to cancel the contract, the seller must notify the buyer whether he intends to repossess or abandon the goods. If the seller fails to pick up the goods within 20 days of cancellation, the buyer can keep the goods without paying for them! From the date goods are delivered, to the end of the 20-day period for the seller to pick up goods after a contract is cancelled, the buyer must take "reasonable" care of the goods.

Some state Home Solicitation Acts provide that if a seller has performed some service for the buyer in connection with a home solicitation sale, the seller will be entitled to demand a nominal "cancellation fee," which usually can be no more than five percent of the cash price of the goods sold, $15, or the amount of cash down payment, whichever is less. Other state Home Solicitation Acts provide that if the seller altered the buyer's property in connection with a sale, he is required to restore the buyer's property to its original condition if the sale is cancelled.

Referral Sales

Many state Home Solicitation Acts also make "referral" sales cancelable. "Referral" sales are a kind of home solicitation sale where the seller offers to give you a rebate or discount if you give him names of other prospective customers and one or more of those persons later buy something from or even meet with the seller. If a seller makes such promises to you in connection with a home solicitation sale, many states allow you to cancel the sale anytime. The law discourages referral sales because the discounts or rebates offered in exchange for the referrals are often phony. Salesmen often fail to notify former customers that a sale resulted from someone the customer referred, and consumers usually have no way to discover that a sale occurred from their referral.

The law discourages referral sales because the discounts or rebates offered in exchange for the referrals are often phony.

Note that many state Home Solicitation Acts require sellers to make far more disclosures than those specified here and imposed by the FTC. Therefore, even if a seller has complied with the FTC rules governing home solicitations, he still might have violated the home solicitation laws imposed by your particular state. Conversely, some state Home Solicitation Acts impose less restrictions on sellers than the restrictions imposed by the FTC. For example, some state Home Solicitation Acts only apply to credit sales. The restrictions imposed by the FTC and outlined in this book always apply, even if the restrictions imposed by your state Home Solicitation Act do not. Check with your attorney general to see if the home solicitation laws of your state are more or less advantageous than the rules imposed on all home solicitors by the FTC.

Mail Orders

Merchandise ordered by mail is a major source of consumer complaints. Most complaints concern delays in delivery. The FTC has issued a rule requiring goods ordered by mail to be shipped within a stated period or, if no time is stated, within 30 days of an order's receipt. If the seller cannot ship the goods within the period stated or within 30 days, the consumer must be offered the opportunity to cancel the order and get his money back.

Merchandise ordered by mail is a major source of consumer complaints.

Unordered Goods

We all have had goods shipped to us unsolicited. Is a consumer responsible for paying for goods shipped to him without his knowledge and permission? Absolutely not!

If you receive merchandise you did not order, you are free to refuse delivery, and you are not responsible for returning the merchandise. If the unsolicited merchandise is addressed to or otherwise intended for you, the law considers such merchandise a gift, and you may use or dispose of it as you see fit. It is unlawful for anyone sending you unsolicited goods to bill you for the goods and if this occurs, you should not only refuse payment, but also complain in writing to your state attorney general, the FTC, and the Direct Mail/Marketing Association, Consumer Relations Department, Six East 43rd Street, New York, New York 10017.

Dance And Health Club Contracts

In addition to regulating telephone and home solicitation sales, many states have enacted statutes regulating particular services which have proven especially troublesome for unwary consumers. Two types of service contracts particularly dangerous for consumers are dance studio and health club contracts. In the past, some studios or clubs obligated their members to make monthly payments for extended periods, sometimes even for a lifetime, even if the member had ceased visiting the studio or club or the studio or club had moved away or gone out of business. Other clubs or studios required their members to prepay huge sums, only to have the clubs or studios move away or go bankrupt. To prevent or at least discourage such abuses, many states have passed statutes regulating dance studio or health club contracts.

Lifetime Payments Banned

The dance studio and health club statutes usually ban lifetime payments and require studio or club memberships to be in writing and conspicuously state the member's total payment obligations. Dance studio and health club laws often set a maximum dollar amount that can be charged for lessons or memberships. The laws also severely restrict the duration of lessons and memberships, as well as any period for financing lessons and memberships. Payment on dance studio and health club contracts is usually strictly conditional on receipt of each lesson or service promised.

Dance studio and health club statutes usually require written notice to consumers that contracts can be canceled within a short period. Generally, consumers may cancel dance con-

Many states have passed statutes regulating dance studio or health club contracts.

tracts within 15 days of signing, whereas health club contracts are usually cancelable within three days of the time they are made. Like most of the rules outlined in this book, the controlling periods may differ from state to state.

When a consumer cancels a contract, dance studios typically must refund within ten days any prepayment made. In contrast, health clubs are usually allowed 30 days to return your money.

Statutes in some states relieve consumers from making payments for dance lessons scheduled after the consumer becomes disabled. If the consumer has prepaid lessons, the studio must refund any portion of the prepayment relating to lessons prevented by the consumer's disability. Surprisingly, many states regulating health clubs do not have a similar rule.

If a studio or club induces you to join by any deception or misrepresentation, or otherwise violates the laws regulating studios or clubs, you usually can cancel your membership and sue for any damages you have incurred. State attorneys general or other law enforcement agencies can prosecute violations of the laws regulating dance studios and health clubs. If you have been victimized by a studio or club, you should complain immediately to law enforcement officials, asking them to take action on your behalf.

Dance studios are sometimes required to file a sizable bond (see page 79) with the state which can be tapped by any consumer damaged by a studio's breach of its contractual or legal obligations. To make a claim on a studio's bond, you often have to sue for reimbursement within a short period after the studio's misconduct. Unfortunately, many states do not require health clubs to post a bond.

In addition to the UCC's rules governing warranties, the federal government has passed laws establishing strict standards for written warranties of limited duration. A written warranty that is only valid for a limited period and does not comply with the federal standards is unlawful, and the person making it is subject to prosecution by the FTC and the United States Attorney.

The federal government has passed laws establishing strict standards for written warranties of limited duration.

This chapter first will explore the federal warranty standards. Most notably, the standards have led to the imposition of informal, out-of-court dispute resolution programs for consumers complaining about automotive defects, and these programs will be explored as well. Finally, this chapter will discuss "lemon laws," the state laws governing resolution of consumer auto complaints which have not been resolved by other available means.

The Federal Warranty Standards

Under federal law, all written warranties of a limited duration for products sold to consumers and valued at $15 or more must:

- Identify the name and address of the person making the warranty (the "warrantor");

- Identify the person to whom the warranty is made (usually, the buyer), unless the warranty applies to every owner during the warranty's term;

- Identify the product (or parts) covered by the warranty and those which are not;

43

- State what the warrantor will do if the product malfunctions or is defective, and for what period of time he will do it;

- State what the buyer must do and what expenses the buyer will bear;

- Provide step-by-step instructions of what the buyer must do to enforce the warranty, including the name of the person who the buyer must notify of his complaint;

- Describe any informal, out-of-court procedure for settling disputes arising out of the purchase and whether the buyer must use such a procedure before suing the warrantor in court;

- Describe any limitations on the duration of any implied warranties, accompanied by the following statement:"Some states do not allow limitations on how long an implied warranty lasts, so the above limitation may not apply to you";

- Describe any exclusions or limitations of the buyer's remedies, accompanied by the following statement:"Some states do not allow the exclusion or limitation of incidental or consequential damages, so the above limitation or exclusion may not apply to you";

- Specify the period of time the warrantor has to perform his duties under the warranty after the buyer notifies him of a defect or other problem;

- State: "This warranty gives you specific legal rights, and you may also have other rights which vary from state to state."

If a product is being sold with a written warranty, the warranty must be made available to the buyer before his purchase.

Full And Limited Warranties

Everyday, we hear of products sold with "limited" warranties. Most consumers probably have no idea what a "limited" warranty really is.

A "limited" warranty is simply one that is not "full." A "full" warranty meets strict minimum standards imposed by the federal government. To qualify as a "full" warranty, a written warranty must:

- State the warrantor will fix the product warranted without charge and within a reasonable time;

- Impose no limitation on the duration of any implied warranties;

- Refrain from excluding or limiting consequential damages for breach of warranty (unless such exclusion or limitation is conspicuously stated on the warranty's face);

A full warranty must impose no limitation on the duration of any implied warranties.

- Permit the owner to elect receipt of a refund or a free replacement if the product (or part thereof) contains a defect which after a reasonable number of attempts the warrantor is unable to fix. If a defective part is replaced, installation of the part must not be charged to the owner;

- Impose no duty on the buyer to return a warranty registration card or similar notice to qualify for warranty protection;

- Impose no limitation on a subsequent owner's right to enforce the warranty during the warranty's stated term.

Written warranties must state, in a conspicuous manner, whether they are limited or full. Products can have both full and limited warranties. For example, some new cars are fully warranted until a year after purchase; thereafter, some of their component parts are warranted to a limited extent for an additional period. No federally imposed restrictions limit the wording of a warranty that is indefinite in duration. Few, if any, warranties, however, are valid forever. On rare occasions, products may carry "lifetime" warranties, indicating they are fully warranted for the buyer's natural life. Such warranties are subject to the federally imposed restrictions. More often, products may carry "unlimited" warranties. Federal law prohibits written warranties from being designated as anything other than full or limited. Therefore, designating a warranty as "unlimited" is a technical violation of the law. Since an "unlimited" warranty implies that it is "full," "unlimited" warranties not meeting the minimum standards of a full warranty are especially unlawful.

Consumer Maintenance

A warrantor does not have to fix or replace warranted products if he can show the product became damaged or nonfunctional because of the buyer's misuse or failure to provide reasonable and necessary maintenance. Since many warranties lapse if the buyer fails to maintain the product as specified in the owner's manual, you should never skip a scheduled maintenance and keep all records relating to this maintenance.

Federal law prohibits warrantors from conditioning any written or implied warranty on the consumer using a particular brand, trade or corporate name product or service, unless the product or service is provided for free. Thus, a car manufacturer or dealer cannot condition the effectiveness of the car's warranty on the buyer's use, for maintenance purposes, of a particular brand-name part, oil or gasoline. Likewise, the manufacturer cannot require your car to be serviced at a particular company's service station or other facility in order for the car's warranty to be effective. While there are some exceptions to these rules, they are few and far between.

The Ban Against Exclusion Of Implied Warranties

One of the best things about getting a written warranty is that this prevents the seller from excluding or changing any implied warranties unless these exclusions or changes are "conscionable," last as long as the written warranty, and are conspicuously stated in the written warranty. Limitations on implied warranties not satisfying federal requirements are unenforceable.

Limitations on implied warranties not satisfying federal requirements are unenforceable.

Used Car Disclosures

The FTC has imposed special restrictions on the warranties made by used car dealers. A used car dealer may not do any of the following:

- Misrepresent the condition of a used vehicle;

- Misrepresent the terms of any warranty offered in connection with the sale of any used vehicle;

- Represent that a used vehicle has a warranty when it does not;

- Fail to disclose, before the sale, that a used vehicle is sold without a warranty; or

- Fail to make available, before the sale, the terms of any written warranty offered in connection with the sale of the used vehicle.

A used car dealer can comply with the special restrictions imposed by the FTC by fully completing the form on page 49 and attaching it to the side windows of all vehicles offered for sale.

Private Rights Of Action

You are entitled to sue a warrantor for breach of any of the rules outlined in this chapter. In such a lawsuit, you may recover all reasonably foreseeable damages you have suffered as well as any attorneys' fees you have paid to prosecute the lawsuit. You should resort to bringing a lawsuit only after you have exhausted all other options to obtain relief.

You should resort to bringing a lawsuit only after you have exhausted all other options to obtain relief.

New Car Dispute Resolution Programs

Federal law encourages sellers warranting their products to establish informal, out-of-court procedures for settling consumer complaints about the products. The auto industry has wholeheartedly embraced the concept of out-of-court dispute resolution. Most car manufacturers have adopted out-of-court programs to resolve consumer complaints, and statutes in many states require consumers encountering car problems to participate in such programs before seeking relief in the courts.

Most informal settlement programs are not run by the automakers or dealers themselves, but instead, by an "independent" third party. Some

BUYER'S GUIDE

FORM BG-1002 NORICK OKLAHOMA CITY

IMPORTANT: Spoken promises are difficult to enforce. Ask the dealer to put all promises in writing. Keep this form.

| VEHICLE MAKE | MODEL | YEAR | VIN NUMBER |

DEALER STOCK NUMBER (Optional)

WARRANTIES FOR THIS VEHICLE:

☐ AS IS - NO WARRANTY

YOU WILL PAY ALL COSTS FOR ANY REPAIRS. The dealer assumes no responsibility for any repairs regardless of any oral statements about the vehicle.

☐ WARRANTY

☐ FULL ☐ LIMITED WARRANTY. The dealer will pay _____% of the labor and _____% of the parts for the covered systems that fail during the warranty period. Ask the dealer for a copy of the warranty document for a full explanation of warranty coverage, exclusions, and the dealer's repair obligations. Under state law, "implied warranties" may give you even more rights.

SYSTEMS COVERED:	DURATION:
_____	_____
_____	_____
_____	_____
_____	_____
_____	_____
_____	_____
_____	_____

☐ SERVICE CONTRACT. A service contract is available at an extra charge on this vehicle. Ask for details as to coverage, deductible, price, and exclusions. If you buy a service contract within 90 days of the time of sale, state law "implied warranties" may give you additional rights.

PRE PURCHASE INSPECTION: ASK THE DEALER IF YOU MAY HAVE THIS VEHICLE INSPECTED BY YOUR MECHANIC EITHER ON OR OFF THE LOT.

SEE THE BACK OF THIS FORM for important additional information, including a list of some major defects that may occur in used motor vehicles.

Below is a list of some major defects that may occur in used motor vehicles.

Frame & Body
Frame-cracks, corrective welds, or rusted through
Dogtracks — bent or twisted frame

Engine
Oil leakage, excluding normal seepage
Cracked block or head
Belts missing or inoperable
Knocks or misses related to camshaft lifters and push rods
Abnormal exhaust discharge

Transmission & Drive Shaft
Improper fluid level or leakage, excluding normal seepage
Cracked or damaged case which is visible
Abnormal noise or vibration caused by faulty transmission or drive shaft
Improper shifting or functioning in any gear
Manual clutch slips or chatters

Differential
Improper fluid level or leakage excluding normal seepage
Cracked or damaged housing which is visible
Abnormal noise or vibration caused by faulty differential

Cooling System
Leakage including radiator
Improperly functioning water pump

Electrical System
Battery leakage
Improperly functioning alternator, generator, battery, or starter

Fuel System
Visible leakage

Inoperable Accessories
Gauges or warning devices
Air conditioner
Heater & Defroster

Brake System
Failure warning light broken
Pedal not firm under pressure (DOT spec.)
Not enough pedal reserve (DOT spec.)
Does not stop vehicle in straight (DOT spec.)
Hoses damaged
Drum or rotor too thin (Mfgr. Specs)
Lining or pad thickness less than 1/32 inch
Power unit not operating or leaking
Structural or mechanical parts damaged

Steering System
Too much free play at steering wheel (DOT specs.)
Free play in linkage more than 1/4 inch
Steering gear binds or jams
Front end aligned improperly (DOT specs.)
Power unit belts cracked or slipping
Power unit fluid level improper

Suspension System
Ball joint seals damaged
Structural parts bent or damaged
Stabilizer bar disconnected
Spring broken
Shock absorber mounting loose
Rubber bushings damaged or missing
Radius rod damaged or missing
Shock absorber leaking or functioning improperly

Tires
Tread depth less than 2/32 inch
Sizes mismatched
Visual damage

Wheels
Visible cracks, damage or repairs
Mounting bolts loose or missing

Exhaust System
Leakage

DEALER _____

ADDRESS _____

SEE FOR COMPLAINTS _____

Receipt of copy Acknowledged _____
(TRANSFEREE'S SIGNATURE - BUYER)

IMPORTANT: The information on this form is part of any contract to buy this vehicle. Removal of this label before consumer purchase (except for purpose of test-driving) is a violation of federal law (16 C.F.R. 445).

settlement programs are more independent than others, for some are industry-sponsored.

Most settlement programs direct the consumer's complaint against the manufacturer instead of the dealer. Generally, the programs attempt to resolve consumer complaints that vehicles are defective or unsafe or that service has been inadequate, overly expensive or ineffective. The programs will not resolve cases involving personal injuries or property damage, nor will they settle disputes about insurance. To participate in most programs, you must still own the car and have regularly used it for personal, rather than business purposes.

Most Settlement Programs Are Free

A consumer participating in an informal settlement program can be awarded a wide range of relief.

Almost all settlement programs are free to the consumer, and some programs boast that consumer complaints are resolved, on average, in less than two months. A consumer participating in an informal settlement program can be awarded a wide range of relief, from nothing to a new vehicle, a refund and/or reimbursement of any repair costs paid. Many programs will not reimburse consumers for any attorneys' fees they have paid, nor will many assess "punitive" damages against the manufacturer.

Most informal settlement programs attempt to settle consumer complaints by suggesting a particular remedy either party is free to accept or reject. Most disputes are settled in this manner. If either party rejects the program's recommended remedy, the vast majority of informal settlement programs offer two additional kinds of procedures: "mediation" and "arbitration." Mediation is a process where an independent third party called a

"Mediator" attempts to persuade the parties to voluntarily settle their differences. Arbitration is a process whereby an independent third party called an "Arbitrator" considers the positions of each party and then rules in favor of one or the other. Mediation nearly always precedes arbitration.

In most informal settlement programs, an arbitration decision only is binding on the manufacturer, not the consumer. Therefore, if the consumer is dissatisfied with the outcome of an arbitration, he can ignore the decision and seek relief in the courts. Unfortunately, evidence of an arbitration usually can be used in court. Thus, an arbitration decision adverse to the consumer may be used by a manufacturer to persuade the judge or jury that the consumer should lose his court case.

Informal settlement programs are of three distinct kinds: those operated by the auto industry, those operated by state government, and those independent of the other two. The three major industry sponsored programs are:

(1) AutoCAP

AutoCAP is operated by the National Automobile Dealer's Association, 8400 Westpark Drive, MacLean, Virginia 22102, (800) 252-6232. AutoCAP offers both mediation and arbitration, and arbitration decisions are not binding on the consumer. Sometimes, AutoCAP arbitration decisions may not be binding on the manufacturer either. Many owners of Acura, Alfa Romeo, Austin Rover, BMW, Fiat, Honda, Infiniti, Isuzu, Jaguar, Mazda, Mitsubishi, Nissan, Rolls-Royce, Saab, Sterling, Volvo and Yugo vehicles can participate in AutoCAP.

If the consumer is dissatisfied with the outcome of an informal arbitration, he can ignore the decision and seek relief in the courts.

(2) Chrysler

Owners of Chrysler, Dodge, Plymouth, Jeep and Eagle vehicles generally participate in mediation and arbitration programs operated by the Chrysler Customer Arbitration Board ("CCAB"), P.O. Box 1718, Detroit, Michigan 48288, (800) 992-1997. Only the dealer or manufacturer is bound by an arbitration decision rendered by the CCAB, not the consumer.

(3) Ford

Most owners of Ford, Mercury and Lincoln vehicles participate in a dispute resolution program operated by the Ford Consumer Appeals Board ("FCAB"), P.O. Box 5120, Southfield, Michigan 48086-5120, (800) 241-8450. Generally, arbitration decisions entered by the FCAB only bind the manufacturer, not the consumer.

Some states, operate or sponsor arbitration and / or mediation programs for their residents.

Some states, including Connecticut, the District of Columbia, Florida, Georgia, Hawaii, Maine, Massachusetts, Montana, New Jersey, New York, Rhode Island, Texas, South Carolina, Vermont and Washington operate or sponsor arbitration and/or mediation programs for their residents. Your state attorney general or consumer affairs office can tell you whether a state program is available and whether its rules are more or less advantageous than those of the private program specified in your warranty.

There are just three dispute resolution programs independent of the government and the auto industry:

(1) AutoLine

AutoLine is sponsored by the Counsel of Better Business Bureaus, 4200 Wilson Boulevard, Arlington, Virginia 22203-1804, (800) 955-5100. The program has both mediation and arbitration services. Owners of Acura, Audi, General Motors, Honda, Infiniti, Nissan, Saab, Saturn and Volkswagen vehicles can usually participate in AutoLine. In a few states, owners of Alfa Romeo, BMW, Isuzu, Jaguar, Mitsubishi, Peugeot, Range Rover, Rolls-Royce, Subaru, Sterling and Maserati vehicles can participate in the program. Your owner's manual, warranty or dealer will tell you whether AutoLine is available as a dispute resolution program for your vehicle. Consumers, unlike manufacturers, are not bound by AutoLine arbitration decisions.

Consumers, unlike manufacturers, are not bound by AutoLine arbitration decisions.

(2) AAA

The American Arbitration Association ("AAA"), with regional offices in most major cities, operates an arbitration and mediation service in which owners of Volvo, Mazda, and Suzuki vehicles can sometimes participate. AAA arbitration decisions usually bind both the manufacturer and the consumer, and consumers may have to pay a fee to participate. Some states, including New York, Massachusetts, Georgia and Hawaii, use AAA to arbitrate government-sponsored dispute resolution programs, and in those instances, owners of most vehicle makes can participate.

(3) AUTOSOLVE

AUTOSOLVE provides mediation and arbitration for Hyundai, Lexus, Porsche and Toyota owners, as well as Subaru owners in a few western states. AUTOSOLVE is sponsored by the American Automobile Association, Box 16, 1000 AAA Drive, Heathrow, Florida, 32746-5064, (800) 477-6583. Only the manufacturer is bound by an AUTOSOLVE arbitration decision.

Of all the consumer complaints submitted to dispute resolution programs, only about 17% reach the arbitration stage.

Of all the consumer complaints submitted to dispute resolution programs, only about 17% reach the arbitration stage. Of those claims that are arbitrated, less than 30% of the consumers obtain a verdict 100% in their favor, although most consumers are satisfied with the result obtained at arbitration.

How To Participate

If you have a complaint about a new car which you are unable to resolve with the dealer or manufacturer, find out from your owner's manual, warranty, dealer or attorney general's office what dispute resolution program applies and write that program for a copy of its rules and procedures, which will tell you what you must do to prosecute your claim. The most common error committed by consumers is their failure to fully document their claim. Therefore, along with a concise, written explanation of your complaint, submit legible copies of all documents and records relating to your claim, including repair bills, troubleshooting reports, payment receipts, recall notices, correspondence, notes of meetings or telephone conversations, and evaluations by independent "experts." Some authorities even suggest you submit physical evidence, like auto parts, if such evidence will best prove your case.

Upon receipt of your fully documented complaint, the dispute resolution program usually will propose a settlement of the dispute. If either party rejects the proposed settlement, the manufacturer will submit a written response to your complaint. If mediation is rejected or proves unsuccessful, an arbitrator may either render a decision based on the written documents provided or may decide the case after each side has presented its case at a hearing. Whether a hearing is allowed or required varies from program to program. Note that you might be required to present your vehicle for inspection as part of any arbitration.

State Lemon Laws

A consumer dissatisfied with the result of an arbitration program has one more course of action at his disposal. He can sue for violation of his state's "Lemon Laws." Lemon Laws are statutes enacted in most states requiring car manufacturers and dealers to either replace a severely flawed vehicle or refund the vehicle's purchase price.

Usually, to bring suit under most state Lemon Laws, you must first complete an arbitration program.

Usually, to bring suit under most state Lemon Laws, you must first complete an arbitration program. To qualify for relief under a Lemon Law, a consumer must prove that during the term of any express warranty covering his vehicle, (1) he reported a malfunction covered by the warranty; (2) the malfunction substantially impairs the vehicle's use and value; and (3) the manufacturer or dealer was unable to fix the malfunction after four or more attempts, or the vehicle was being repaired for 30 days or more during the warranty period. If such facts are proven, the consumer will be entitled to a replacement vehicle or, upon his return of the vehicle, to a refund of its purchase price, less a reasonable allowance for the vehicle's mileage.

Most Lemon Laws give consumers no right to sue for defects or malfunctions not substantially impairing the use and market value of their vehicles. Thus, you would have a hard time convincing a judge or jury that you are entitled to a new car simply because the car dealer has been unable to fix an irritating clicking sound that occurs whenever you brake.

You also are not entitled to any relief under the Lemon Laws if the malfunction results from your own abuse, neglect or unauthorized modification of the vehicle. An unauthorized modification is a change to the vehicle that the dealer or manufacturer has neither performed nor recommended.

Most Lemon Laws require you to bring suit against the manufacturer or dealer within six months after your warranty expires or one year after you first get the vehicle, whichever is earlier. To find out the controlling period in your state, check with the office of your state attorney general, or call or write the Center For Auto Safety, 2001 South Street, N.W. , Washington, D.C. 20009, (202) 328-7700.

CHAPTER SIX:
CONSUMER CREDIT PROTECTION

Your Right To Accurate Credit Information

The terms "credit," "borrow" and "finance" all mean the same thing. When you "finance" a purchase, or purchase goods "on credit," you simply are borrowing some or all of the money required to make the purchase. You can finance purchases from the seller or a third party. The person lending you the money for a purchase is called a "creditor."

Thomas Jefferson considered credit purchases such a curse he lobbied Congress to prohibit them. With a federal budget deficit now well over a trillion dollars and most consumers in debt up to their ears, we might well wish Jefferson's efforts to abolish credit purchases had been successful. Whether for good or ill, however, buying things on credit is an important part of our everyday lives. Indeed, a consumer's ability to obtain credit is of such great value, and entails such great risks, that Congress has enacted numerous federal statutes to protect consumers involved in many kinds of credit transactions. The highlights of the most important of these are discussed below.

> *Thomas Jefferson considered credit purchases such a curse he lobbied Congress to prohibit them.*

Credit Disclosures

Federal law requires most businesses selling or renting goods on credit, or companies financing consumer purchases under $25,000 in value, to make various disclosures about what the cost of any credit provided will be. Generally, the disclosures must be made before the sale or rental contract ("lease") is signed, as well as with every periodic billing statement sent the consumer. The required disclosures vary, depending upon whether the transaction is a purchase or a lease.

Purchase Disclosures

The most important disclosure required in a transaction where you purchase goods on credit is the "finance charge." The finance charge is the total sum being assessed you for the credit provided. In addition to interest, the finance charge usually includes fees for extending the credit (often called "points" or "loan fees"), fees to service the consumer's credit account, fees to investigate the consumer's credit history, and/or fees to cover the cost of any insurance purchased by the creditor to protect him against the consumer's default.

Many creditors require consumers to buy some form of "credit insurance," which is insurance that will pay off the consumer's credit balance if the consumer can no longer pay for the goods purchased, either because the goods have become lost or damaged or because the consumer dies or becomes ill. The premiums charged for the credit insurance must be included in the finance charge unless the creditor notifies the consumer this insurance is optional and specifies what the cost of the insurance will be. No charges for credit insurance may be billed a consumer unless the consumer signs or initials a request for such insurance.

No charges for credit insurance may be billed a consumer unless the consumer signs or initials a request for such insurance.

Steer clear of credit insurance! It is usually a very poor value, and often ends up costing far more than the goods whose payment the insurance is supposed to protect.

The second most important disclosure required in a financed purchase transaction is the Annual Percentage Rate, or "APR." The APR is the cost of the credit extended on a yearly basis. The APR is expressed in terms of a percentage of the amount financed or borrowed, including any finance charges.

Creditors also must disclose the amount being financed, the total of all payments required to pay off the amount financed, and the total sales price of the goods, inclusive of all credit charges. Usually, the name of the creditor must be identified, as well as the means of calculating the opening balance, credits, late charges, and any remaining amount owed. Creditors also must specify any rules relating to prepayment procedures or required deposits, and also must identify whether any "grace" or "free ride period" exists.

Most credit cards have a 25 to 30 day grace period.

A grace or free ride period is the time within which a balance must be paid to avoid being assessed periodic finance charges. Most credit cards have a 25 to 30 day grace period. So long as you pay for items charged within the grace period allowed, your purchase will be treated as if you had paid cash and you will not be charged finance charges on the purchase. Note that some credit cards have no grace period.

Lease Disclosures

The disclosures required to be made by a business leasing (renting) you goods are markedly different from those required to be made in a transaction in which you have purchased goods or services on credit. Before a lease transaction is signed, the "lessor" (the person renting you the goods) must provide you with a dated, written statement containing the following items, among others:

- A brief description of the leased property;
- The total amount of any payments, including the amount of any refundable

security deposits, advance payments, or trade-in allowance to be paid by, or credited to, the lessee (the renter);

- The number, amount and dates of any payments required, together with the total amount of the periodic payments;
- The total amount payable during the lease term for government fees, registration, certificates of title, license fees or taxes;
- The individually itemized total of all other charges payable by the lessor which are not included in the periodic payments;
- A brief identification of the type and amount of any insurance provided by the lessor or required to be obtained by the lessee;
- A statement identifying any express warranties available to the lessee;
- The party responsible for maintaining or servicing the leased goods, together with a brief description of what that responsibility is and a statement of "reasonable" standards of what constitutes "wear and tear" for which the lessee shall not be responsible;
- A description of whether the lessor will have a lien on the goods to secure prompt payment;
- The amount (or method of determining the amount) of any late charge;
- A statement of whether and when the lessee has the option to purchase the leased goods and the price (or method of determining the price) for such a purchase;

- A statement of the conditions under which the lessor or lessee may end the lease before expiration of the lease term and the amount (or method of determining the amount) of any penalty for early termination;

- A statement whether the lessee is liable for the difference between the "estimated value" of the property (usually set at the beginning of the lease) and its actual value at early termination or the end of the lease term;

- If the lessee's liability is based on any estimated value of the leased property, a statement that the lessee may obtain at the end of the lease term, or at early termination, a professional appraisal of the property's value by an independent appraiser acceptable by both parties and that this appraisal is binding on all parties.

Credit Cards

Have you ever wondered why credit card issuers regularly send unsolicited letters saying you have been "approved" for a credit card but nevertheless require you to fill out an application before your "approved" card will be sent? This apparent contradiction results from an obscure federal statute prohibiting credit cards from being issued except in response to a request or an application. The prohibition does not apply to the issuance of credit cards in renewal of or substitution for a card you already possess.

Federal statutes prohibit credit cards from being issued except in response to a request or an application.

Credit Card Liability

Federal law provides that you are not liable for any unauthorized use of your credit card after you notify the card's issuer, by telephone or written communication, that the card has been lost or stolen. The law also provides that even if you fail to report a lost or stolen card, you are only liable for up to a maximum of $50 in charges incurred by an unauthorized user. Credit card issuers rarely contest a consumer's claim that a charge was unauthorized since the most they can recover is $50 and the law presumes the charge was unauthorized unless the card issuer can prove otherwise.

Even if you fail to report a lost or stolen card, you are only liable for up to a maximum of $50 in charges incurred by an unauthorized user.

Right To Withhold Payment

Purchasing goods or services by credit card is preferable over cash or check transactions because in most instances, you can withhold payment on a credit card transaction if you are dissatisfied with the goods or services purchased. If you already have paid for services or goods in cash, the seller has far less motivation to satisfy your concerns than if he was still waiting for payment!

Generally, you can withhold payment on a credit card purchase if (1) the amount purchased exceeds $50; (2) you have made a good faith attempt to resolve the problem; and (3) the transaction involved occurred within (or within 100 miles of) the state where you live. You can withhold payment without complying with conditions (2) and (3) above if you ordered the goods or services from a mail solicitation sent by or on behalf of your credit card issuer.

If you have a credit balance on your credit account at the time you notify a credit card issuer you are withholding payment because you are dissatisfied with the goods or services purchased, the card issuer cannot apply your credit balance to satisfy the charge for which you are withholding payment, unless a court order allowing it to take such action is first obtained. Moreover, if you refuse to pay a particular credit card charge because of dissatisfaction with the goods or services about which the charge relates, neither your credit card issuer nor the seller can report the amount withheld as delinquent on your "credit report" (see page 65) until the disputed amount is either settled or you are adjudged to owe it by a court.

A card issuer cannot aply your credit balance to satisfy any charge you dispute.

Property Returns

If a seller in a credit card transaction accepts the return of purchased goods or forgives a charge for services, he must notify the card issuer to credit the consumer's account for the appropriate amount refunded within seven business days. Within three business days of receiving a refund notice, the card issuer must credit the card holder's account with the amount of the refund.

Billing Errors

If you believe your credit account statement contains any kind of a billing error, you must immediately notify the creditor of the problem. Within 30 days of receiving such notice, the creditor must acknowledge receipt of the billing error notice. Within 90 days of receiving your notice of a billing error, the creditor must either correct the billing error as requested, or make a reasonable investigation and explain why either no correction or only a partial correction is appropriate. Upon receipt of this explanation, you can ask the creditor to send you documentation supporting his position.

If your credit agreement requires you to make a minimum monthly payment, you may withhold any portion of the minimum payment that you believe is related to a billing error. If a billing error was made, the creditor must credit your account for any amount improperly billed, plus any finance charges or late payment charges imposed as a result of the erroneous billing. A creditor can threaten to report or actually report the consumer as delinquent on his payment obligations, despite the consumer's failure to pay on grounds of a billing error, so long as the creditor (1) has fully investigated the consumer's complaint; (2) gives the consumer an additional ten days to pay any undisputed amount due; and (3) notifies the consumer, within 90 days of the consumer's complaint, that the complaint is without merit. However, if the consumer then notifies the creditor that the amounts claimed are erroneously billed, any delinquency reported by the creditor must reflect that the amounts reported as delinquent are disputed. If a creditor violates these rules, he forfeits up to $50 in charges for each item indicated by the consumer to be a billing error.

You may withhold any portion of your minimum payment that you believe is related to a billing error.

Creditor Liability For Improper Disclosure Or Conduct

Creditors intentionally failing to make the disclosures required for a financed purchase transaction can be sued for all actual damage suffered by the buyer, as well as twice the amount of any finance charge assessed. Persons injured by lessors who intentionally fail to make the disclosures required in a lease transaction can recover 25% of the total amount of monthly payments under the lease contract, up to a maximum of $1000, in addition to their actual damages. Both buyers and lessees can recover any court costs and attorneys' fees they have paid to prosecute their lawsuit. Suit must be brought within one year of a creditor's violation.

The FTC also is authorized to prosecute violations of the consumer credit laws. Therefore, you should always ask the FTC for help in addressing what you believe to be a violation of the consumer credit acts.

Credit Reporting Rules

Anyone who has purchased goods or services on credit, or even leased goods, has a "credit report." A credit report is a detailed itemization of most of a consumer's credit transactions, listing the date, amount and kind of each transaction as well as whether the consumer timely made all payments required. These reports are compiled by "credit reporting agencies" and often are used by merchants and lessors to decide whether a consumer is a satisfactory risk to receive credit.

Anyone who has purchased goods or services on credit, or even leased goods, has a "credit report."

Because an inaccurate credit record may unfairly deprive a consumer of credit, Congress has placed strict limitations on use of credit reports. These limitations are set forth below.

Who May Get A Credit Report

Anyone can obtain a consumer's credit report so long as the person requesting the report is involved in a business transaction involving the consumer. Thus, any merchant or lessor from whom a consumer requests credit can obtain the consumer's credit report. Consumers can request credit reports on themselves simply by forwarding a written request to one of the three major credit reporting agencies: (1) Credit Data Of America, (2) CBI/Equifax, and (3) TRW. The telephone number and address for each of these agencies is in the Yellow Pages of your telephone directory under "Credit Reporting Agencies."

What Credit Reports Cannot Disclose

Consumers can request credit reports on themselves simply by forwarding a written request to one of the three major credit reporting agencies.

Generally, federal law prohibits credit reports from containing adverse information more than seven years old. For example, a report cannot mention lawsuits, judgments, accounts placed for collection, arrests, indictments, criminal convictions, tax liens or most bankruptcies which occurred more than seven years before the report was made. Chapter 11 bankruptcies (reorganizations) can be reported until they are ten years old, and all adverse information can be disclosed in a report made in connection with a transaction involving at least $50,000 or the purchase of life insurance.

Report Disclosure

A report of your credit history cannot be obtained unless you are notified that such a report is being requested. Such a notice must be

66

in writing and mailed or delivered to you within three days of when the report was first requested. The notice also must disclose that you can demand the party requesting the report to completely and accurately explain the nature and scope of the investigation being conducted.

A creditor must tell you if he denies you credit or increases the cost of the credit you have requested because of adverse information contained in your credit report. He must also provide you with the name and address of the reporting agency compiling the credit report.

If within 30 days of your receipt of notice that there exists adverse information in your credit report, you then request a copy of your credit report from the reporting agency identified as having provided the adverse information, the agency must provide you with a copy of the report free of charge. A consumer requesting a report after the 30-day period may be charged a "reasonable" fee for a copy.

A creditor must tell you if he denies you credit or increases the cost of the credit you have requested because of adverse information contained in your credit report.

Correcting Erroneous Information

A consumer discovering inaccurate information in his credit report can (and should) notify the reporting agency of the inaccuracy. After receiving this notice, the agency must investigate the consumer's claim, unless the agency reasonably believes the claim is frivolous. If the agency discovers the contested information is inaccurate or simply cannot be verified, it must delete the information from its report. On the other hand, if the agency determines the consumer's complaint is not valid, the consumer can submit a written statement of up to 100 words describing why he believes the information reported is inaccurate. Unless the reporting agency believes the consumer's statement is frivolous, it must include the statement (or summary) in its report on the consumer. And at the consumer's request, the agency also must furnish copies of any deletion or explanation of information to all persons identified by the consumer who received copies of the consumer's credit report within the past six months.

Reporting Agency Liability

A consumer victimized by a reporting agency's intentional violation of the duties described in this book can sue for actual and punitive damages, as well as all sums incurred by the consumer for court costs and attorneys' fees. Reporting agencies which negligently, rather than intentionally, violate their legal duties are liable only for the consumer's actual damages, court costs and attorneys' fees, not punitive damages. Generally, a consumer must bring a lawsuit for violation of credit reporting laws within two years of the reporting agency's misconduct. The FTC also can prosecute reporting agencies which violate their reporting obligations, and consumers injured by an agency's unlawful reporting practices should complain about such conduct to the FTC.

Generally, a consumer must bring a lawsuit for violation of credit reporting laws within two years of the reporting agency's misconduct.

Credit Discrimination

Businesses cannot deny or charge you more for credit because of your race, religion, national origin, sex, marital status or age. You also cannot be denied or charged extra for credit solely because you are receiving some form of public assistance or welfare. However, businesses evaluating your creditworthiness can inquire about your marital status for nondiscriminatory purposes. For example, in some western "community property" states, certain contracts are not enforceable against a married couple unless both spouses sign the contract documents. Thus, a business extending credit in a community property state may ask whether you are married. Likewise, businesses can inquire about your age or receipt of public assistance if these inquiries are not made for discriminatory purposes, but instead to determine whether you are incapable, due to advanced age or poverty, of repaying any credit extended.

Businesses can ask you where you live and if you are a U.S. citizen. They also can ask the number and ages of your children and even what it costs you to care for them. However, creditors cannot ask about birth control practices or your intentions or ability to bear children. In most instances, creditors also may not ask whether any income shown on your credit application comes from alimony, child support or separate maintenance payments. In general, creditors may not request any information about your spouse or ex-spouse unless (1) your spouse or ex-spouse is going to use or be responsible for your credit account; (2) you live in a "community property" state; or (3) you are relying on your spouse or ex-spouse to repay your credit account. If you are recently divorced or retired, and nothing suggests that you are unwilling or unable to continue paying on an already established credit account, your creditor cannot require you to reapply for credit, change the terms of your account, or terminate your account.

Creditors cannot ask about birth control practices or your intentions or ability to bear children.

Notice Of Approval Or Rejection

Creditors have 30 days to notify consumers whether their credit applications have been approved. The notice usually must be in writing and, among other things, must either state the specific reasons for any denial of credit or, at the very least, inform the consumer he is entitled to a detailed explanation of any denial within 30 days of requesting that explanation.

Creditor Liability

Creditors have 30 days to notify consumers whether their credit applications have been approved.

Consumers can sue creditors who violate the federal anti-discrimination rules for actual damages plus up to $10,000 in punitive damages! Consumers also can recover their court costs and attorneys' fees and demand the credit they requested be provided. Generally, a lawsuit must be brought within two years of a violation.

The FTC prosecutes violations of the federal anti-discrimination laws. Report any unlawful discrimination to the FTC so the agency can address it.

CHAPTER SEVEN:
UNFAIR DEBT COLLECTION PRACTICES

Nearly everyone has been badgered by debt collectors at one time or another. Apparently, one too many Congressmen was badgered as well, for in the late 1970s, Congress enacted a series of statutes collectively called the "Fair Debt Collection Practices Act," which strictly limit what debt collectors can do to collect debts.

In general, the Fair Debt Collection Practices Act, or "FDCPA," only applies to firms that collect the debts of others. Thus, no federal law limits the collection practices of creditors themselves. Only persons not affiliated with the creditor, but attempting to collect a debt on his behalf, are subject to the FDCPA. The FDCPA usually does not apply to the government, nor does it apply to most attorneys collecting debts on behalf of their clients. This chapter will outline your basic rights under the FDCPA.

> *Debt collectors attempting to find debtors cannot tell persons other than the debtor that the debtor owes money.*

Prohibition Against Defamation

Under the FDCPA, debt collectors attempting to find debtors cannot tell persons other than the debtor that the debtor owes money. Debt collectors cannot communicate with a debtor's friends, relatives or acquaintances by postcard, nor can debt collectors use any language or symbol, in written communications to third parties, that indicates the debt collector is in the debt collection business or that he is attempting to collect a debt. All a debt collector can tell third parties is his name and that he is confirming or correcting information about a consumer's location. Debt collectors can have only one contact with each third party contacted to locate the debtor.

Prohibited Communications

Unless a debtor consents, a debt collector cannot telephone or directly call upon a debtor before 8 o'clock a.m. or after 9 o'clock p.m. local time. Unless a debtor consents, debt collectors cannot contact a debtor at his work, and if the debt collector knows the debtor has an attorney, he must direct all inquiries to the attorney, unless the attorney fails to respond within a reasonable period of time. Once a debt collector knows where a debtor is, he cannot communicate with anyone other than the creditor, the debtor or their attorneys, unless the debtor agrees otherwise.

> *Unless a debtor consents, a debt collector cannot telephone or directly call upon a debtor before 8 o'clock a.m. or after 9 o'clock p.m. local time.*

If a debtor notifies a debt collector, in writing, that the debtor either refuses to pay the debt or wishes the debt collector to cease communicating with him, the debt collector must cease communicating with the debtor. The debt collector can notify the debtor, however, that the creditor intends to take certain specified action.

Under no circumstances can a debt collector harass, oppress or abuse you. Threats to harm the person, reputation or property of anyone are unlawful, as is the use of profane or abusive language. Debt collectors cannot threaten to tell third parties of your debts, nor can they repeatedly telephone you to harass you into paying a debt.

Misleading Representations

Debt collectors are also strictly prohibited from making any false, deceptive or misleading statements to collect a debt. Thus, debt collectors cannot falsely state or imply that they are connected with the government or a credit reporting agency, nor can they falsely state the character, amount or validity of any debt. Debt collectors cannot falsely state or imply they are attorneys or that nonpayment of the debt will result in your arrest or imprisonment. In general, debt collectors cannot threaten to take any action they cannot legally take or do not intend to take.

Debt collectors cannot falsely state or imply that the debtor committed a crime or acted disgracefully. Debt collectors cannot communicate or threaten to communicate false information about the debtor. They also cannot falsely represent the nature of documents sent to the debtor. In other words, a debt collector cannot falsely state that written payment demands earlier sent to the debtor are court papers.

Unfair Collection Practices

The FDCPA bans debt collectors from using "unfair or unconscionable means to collect or attempt to collect a debt." Among other things, this ban prohibits debt collectors from collecting amounts not owed or telephoning the debtor collect under false pretenses, such as getting the debtor to accept a collect call by stating the debtor has won a prize. And in most instances, a debt collector cannot accept as payment checks post-dated by more than five days.

Debt Notices

Federal law requires a debt collector to send the debtor a written notice containing five items of information within five days after the collector first contacts the debtor. The notice must contain:

Debt collectors cannot falsely state or imply that the debtor committed a crime or acted disgracefully.

(1) the amount of the debt;

(2) the name of the creditor to whom the debt is owed;

(3) a statement that unless the debtor, within 30 days after receipt of the notice, disputes the validity of the debt, or any portion of it, the debt will be assumed valid by the collector;

(4) a statement that if the debtor notifies the debt collector in writing within the 30-day period that the debt, or any portion of it, is disputed, the debt collector will obtain verification of the debt and copies of the documents verifying the debt will be mailed to the debtor by the debt collector; and

(5) a statement that, upon the debtor's written request within the 30-day period, the debt collector will provide the debtor with the name and address of the original creditor, if different from the current creditor.

If a debtor fails to request verification of the debt, this cannot be considered an admission he owes the debt. However, if the debtor requests verification of the debt or the name and address of the original creditor, the debt collector must cease efforts to collect the debt until he verifies the debt or the name and address of the original creditor and mails verification of the debt or the name and address of the original creditor to the debtor. Thus, always request verification of the debt. In instances where you simply need more time to pay off a debt, requesting verification will buy you some breathing room.

If a debtor fails to request verification of the debt, this cannot be considered an admission he owes the debt.

Liability For Violating The FDCPA

Debt collectors who intentionally violate the rules prescribed by the FDCPA can be sued by the debtor for the debtor's actual damages, punitive damages of up to $1000, court costs and any attorneys' fees incurred by the debtor during the lawsuit. Generally, suit must be brought within one year of the debt collector's unlawful conduct. The FTC also can prosecute debt collectors for violations of the FDCPA, and consumers victimized by a debt collector's unlawful acts should complain to the FTC without delay.

No set of uniform statutes governs businesses providing "services," as opposed to "goods." Therefore, consumers have no special rights of recourse against most service providers, other than those provided by the common law. However, state statutes usually regulate the activities of two particular kinds of service providers: "professionals" and "contractors." While the statutes regulating the conduct of professionals and contractors vary from state to state, they often have many elements in common. This chapter will highlight the most important rights commonly provided consumers by the statutes regulating the behavior of professionals and contractors. Thereafter, other rights unique to contracting with professionals and contractors will be discussed.

Who Is A Professional Or Contractor

Originally, the only people who qualified as "professionals" were doctors, lawyers and clergymen. As mankind's knowledge expanded, however, so did the number of professions. Today, a "professional" is anyone who provides a service requiring advanced education and skill that is applied in a primarily mental, as opposed to physical, manner. Architects, accountants, chiropractors, nurses, pharmacists, insurance agents, private investigators, psychologists, stock brokers, real estate agents and veterinarians are but a few of the many professionals with whom consumers contract daily.

> *A "professional" is anyone who provides a service requiring advanced education and skill that is applied in a primarily mental, as opposed to physical, manner.*

Like professionals, contractors often have advanced education or skill. Yet, a contractor's skill is applied in a primarily physical, rather than intellectual, fashion and most often relates in some way to the improvement of a building or other structure. Home builders, electricians, plumbers, masons, landscapers, carpet layers and roofers are all "contractors," to name but a few.

Licensing And Regulation

Nearly every state has enacted statutes regulating how certain groups of professionals or contractors can do business. The statutes usually establish separate oversight agencies charged with licensing and regulating particular groups of professionals or contractors.

Contractors, as a whole, are generally licensed and regulated by a state "Registrar of Contractors," while architects, engineers, geologists and surveyors are usually overseen by a state "Board of Technical Registration." Accountants are overseen by a state "Board of Accounting," chiropractors by a state "Board of Chiropractic Examiners," doctors by a "State Board of Medical Examiners," and dentists by a state "Board of Dentistry." Real estate agents and insurance salesmen often are licensed and regulated by separate state departments (real estate and insurance). Typically, lawyers are licensed and regulated by the State Bar Association, which itself often reports to the State Supreme Court. Your state attorney general's office, or Department of Administration, can tell you what agency regulates a particular group of contractors or professionals. The agencies themselves can provide you with copies of all statutes or regulations governing the conduct of their particular licensees. In general, the regulations require licensees to act honestly, competently and in accordance with technical standards established by the regulating agency.

Consumers injured by the acts of a professional or contractor often can obtain relief by complaining to the agency responsible for licensing and regulating the professional or contractor. Most agencies can suspend or revoke the license of a professional or contractor acting unlawfully or unethically or otherwise injuring the public. Agencies also can order their licensees to cure any harm caused. Most contractors and professionals will go out of their way to accommodate a dissatisfied client to reduce the risk of the client seeking suspension or revocation of their license.

Recovery Funds

Many statutes regulating the conduct of contractors and professionals allow consumers to recover damages caused by a professional or contractor from a pool of monies called a "recovery fund." Typically, a separate recovery fund is established for each profession and category of contractor. The funds are usually underwritten by license renewal fees.

Most contractors and professionals will go out of their way to accommodate a dissatisfied client.

The amount payable from a recovery fund is often limited to $15,000, although a few funds allow recoveries of $50,000 or more. Generally, recovery funds can be reached only after (1) a court finds the professional or contractor guilty of violating established statutes or regulations and (2) the consumer verifies he is unable to obtain reimbursement for his damages from any source other than the recovery fund.

Most recovery funds only will honor claims made within a short period (often two years) of the misconduct. Thus, you should properly make a claim against a recovery fund at the earliest possible moment. Claims are usually made by filing a lawsuit against the contractor or professional and including a claim in that lawsuit for reimbursement from the appropriate fund. Claim procedures vary greatly from state to state, however. To find out how to make a claim against a particular recovery fund, contact the agency responsible for licensing the contractor or professional in question.

Bonds

A "bond" is a sum of cash (or a promise by an insurer or other third party to pay a cash sum), which can be reached to satisfy the claims of injured persons. Most contractors, and some professionals, are required by statute to post bonds to ensure the faithful and diligent performance of their work.

Most contractors, and some professionals, are required by statute to post bonds to ensure the faithful and diligent performance of their work.

Bonds posted by professionals are usually in identical amounts. For example, people licensed to conduct lie detector tests often have to post bonds in the amount of $5000. In contrast, the amount of bond required to be posted by contractors varies greatly, depending upon the kind of work the contractor does and the amount of his annual sales.

Contractors with annual sales of $10,000,000 or more might have to post a bond of $50,000-$100,000. However, contractors doing similar work but having annual sales of less than $150,000 may be required to post only a $2,500 bond. Because the amount of available bond money often is not uniform among contractors, even among those performing similar work, you should always ask a contractor the amount of his bond. Do not hire a contractor whose bond is less than the cost of the work to be performed.

Consumers seeking recovery against a posted bond usually must raise such claims in a lawsuit against the contractor or professional and any third party (usually an insurance company) responsible for paying on the bond. Consumers suing on a bond often can obtain an award sufficient to cover their damages as well as court costs and attorneys' fees. Like lawsuits against recovery funds, lawsuits against bonds must be filed within a short period (usually two years) after the contractor or professional's misconduct. The agency regulating the contractor or professional can tell you exactly when and how to make a claim on a bond.

The agency regulating the contractor or professional can tell you exactly when and how to make a claim on a bond.

Note that if the contractor or professional in question is a major bungler, and other people have made (or are making) claims on his bond, little or no bond money may be available to satisfy your claim. This is because previous claims may have depleted the bond. Most regulatory agencies will tell you if any claims have been made on their licensee's bond, and how much bond money is currently available to satisfy your claim.

Special Common Law Rights

In addition to the rights given consumers by the statutes imposing licensing and regulatory restrictions on professionals and contractors, the common law provides consumers with certain special protections as well. The most important protections are a consumer's remedies for "negligence" and "breach of fiduciary duty."

Negligence

Contractors and professionals can be sued for their "negligence," that is, their failure to act as would a reasonably careful practitioner of their craft in like circumstances. A claim for negligence exists so long as the person sued has acted carelessly and that carelessness has caused the consumer damage. In most states, claims for negligence must be brought within two years of the negligent acts.

Negligence Damages Need Not Be Foreseeable

The damages collectible for negligent behavior are potentially greater than those recoverable for breach of contract. This is because damages recoverable for negligence do not have to be "foreseeable," as they must to be recoverable under a breach of contract theory. The only restriction on the damages recoverable for negligence is the damages must be a consequence of the negligence, and not result from any intervening cause.

Suppose you hire a plumber to unclog your sink. While unclogging your sink, the plumber negligently breaks a water line, flooding your house and ruining many priceless antiques. Under a negligence theory of recovery, the plumber would be liable for the ruined antiques, even if he was unaware of their great value.

Suppose further that in the midst of the flood, you manage to rescue some of your household possessions before they become damaged, but while enroute with these possessions to a stor-

Contractors and professionals can be sued for their "negligence," that is, their failure to act as would a reasonably careful practitioner of their craft in like circumstances.

81

age facility, the goods become damaged in a traffic accident. Even under a negligence theory of recovery, the plumber causing the flood would not be liable for the goods damaged in the traffic accident, for the damage did not result from his negligence but instead from the accident which was an intervening cause.

Fiduciary Duty

A "fiduciary duty" is an obligation imposed by the common law on any service provider whose client places faith, confidence and trust upon his judgment or advice. Most professionals, and some contractors, owe fiduciary duties to their clients. Professionals and contractors owing fiduciary duties to their clients are prohibited from lying to, taking unfair advantage of, or otherwise injuring their clients for selfish reasons.

Persons violating their fiduciary duties are liable to their clients for any damages caused. In many states, a breach of fiduciary duty qualifies as a form of fraud, entitling the injured party to both actual as well as punitive damages. Lawsuits for breach of fiduciary duties usually must be brought within two years of the misconduct.

E & O insurance pays damages caused by the insured party's negligent acts.

E & O Insurance

Most professionals and some contractors carry "Errors and Omission" insurance, often called "E & O" insurance for short. E & O insurance pays damages caused by the insured party's negligent acts. Consumers injured by the negligent acts of a professional or contractor may be able to obtain compensation from the negligent party's E & O insurer, even if the negligent party is bankrupt.

As a rule, E & O insurance does not pay damages for fraudulent activity or breach of fiduciary duty. Consumers should think twice before accusing professionals or contractors of fraudulent activity, for these allegations may give the E & O insurer an excuse for refusing to pay any damages.

Generally, you should make a claim on a professional or contractor's E & O insurance policy after you have hired a lawyer. Usually, claims are made before filing any lawsuit.

Private Associations

In addition to those remedies provided consumers by statutes, the common law, and even E & O insurance, consumers also may have special rights against professionals and contractors through the many private associations to which professionals and contractors belong. For example, nearly all American lawyers belong to the American Bar Association, or "ABA." Though not affiliated with the government, the ABA requires its members to abide by a code of ethics, and members found violating the code may be expelled or otherwise disciplined. Thus, consumers victimized by an ABA member's misconduct can ask the ABA for help, as well as the state agency (usually the state bar association) responsible for regulating attorney behavior.

Remember that in addition to private organizations which have a national membership, there are state organizations which may be able to help too. A list of some of the largest private associations regulating the conduct of professionals and contractors follows, but remember, your state probably has similar organizations which you should also contact:

Generally, you should make a claim on a professional or contractor's E & O insurance policy after you have hired a lawyer.

Accountants

American Institute of
Certified Public
Accountants
1211 Avenue of the
Americas
New York, NY 10036-8775
(212) 575-6209

Chiropractors

American Chiropractic
Association
1701 Clarendon Boulevard
Arlington, VA 22209
(703) 276-8800
 or
International
Chiropractors Association
1110 North Glebe Road
Suite 1000
Arlington, VA 22201
(703) 528-5000

Commodity Brokers

National Futures
Association
200 West Madison Street
Chicago, IL 60606-3447
(312) 781-1410
(800) 621-3570
(toll free outside IL)

Dentists

American Dental
Association
211 East Chicago Avenue
Chicago, IL 60611-2678
(800) 621-8099

Doctors

American Medical
Association
515 North State Street
Chicago, IL 60610
(312) 464-5000

Electricians

Independent Electrical
Contractors (Non-union)
P.O. Box 10378
Alexandria, VA 22310
(703) 549-7351
or
National Electrical
Contractors Association
(Union)
7315 Wisconsin Avenue
Bethesda, MD 20814
(301) 657-3110

Financial Planners

Association of Financial
Planning
Two Concourse Parkway
Suite 800
Atlanta, GA 30328
or
Institute of Certified
Financial Planners
3443 South Galena,
Suite 190
Denver, CO 80231-5093
(303) 751-7600

Home Builders

National Association of
Home Builders
15th and M Streets, N.W.
Washington, DC 20005
(800) 368-5242

Insurance Agents

American Council of Life
Insurance
1001 Pennsylvania Ave. N.W.
Washington, DC 20004-2599
(800) 942-4242

Lawyers

The American Bar
Association Standing
Committee on Dispute
Resolution
1800 M Street, N.W. , Suite
790
Washington, DC 20036
(202) 331-2258

Mortgage Bankers And Title Companies

Mortgage Bankers
Association of America
1125 15th Street, N.W. ,
7th Floor
Washington, DC 20015
(202) 861-1929

Real Estate Agents

National Association of
Realtors
777 14th Street, N.W.
Washington, DC 20005
(202) 383-1000

Stock Brokers

National Association of
Securities Dealers
33 Whitehall Street, 11th
Floor
New York, NY 10004
(212) 858-4000

Travel Agents

American Society of Travel
Agents, Inc.
P.O. Box 23992
Washington, DC 20026-
3992
(703) 739-2782

Many of the associations listed offer arbitration and mediation programs to resolve consumer complaints against their members. In a few instances, consumers may have to complete arbitration programs before becoming eligible to sue the offending professional or contractor in court.

CHAPTER NINE:
HOW TO COMPLAIN AND SUE

Whenever you are displeased about a purchase or a service, you should first complain in a calm and friendly manner to the business providing you the product or service. You can usually obtain satisfaction by way of a simple telephone call or personal visit.

> *You can usually obtain satisfaction by way of a simple telephone call or personal visit.*

If your calls or visits do not resolve the problem, write the business a letter that details your complaint and requests specific relief. The following is a sample complaint letter recommended by the U.S. Office of Consumer Affairs:

(Your address)

(Date)

(Name of Contact Person)
(Title)
(Company Name)
(Address)

(Dear Contact Person):

On (date), I purchased (or had repaired) a (name of the product with serial or model number or service performed). I made this purchase at (location, date and other important details of the transaction).

Unfortunately, your product (or service) has not performed well (or the service was inadequate) because (state the problem).

Therefore, to resolve the problem, I would appreciate your (state the specific action you want). Enclosed are copies (copies, not originals) of my records (receipts, guarantees, canceled checks, contracts, model and serial numbers, and any other documents).

I look forward to your reply and a resolution to my problem, and will wait (set a time limit) before seeking third-party assistance. Please contact me at the above address or by phone at (home or office number with area code).

Sincerely,

(Your name)

(Your account number, if any)

The sample letter emphasizes that you should keep the originals of any documents relating to the transaction since some courts only allow original documents to be used as evidence. It is best to mail your complaint letter by certified mail. This accomplishes two objectives. First, it documents that the business has received the letter. Second, it alerts the business that you consider the matter serious.

If your complaint letter falls on deaf ears, you should write the FTC, any applicable regulatory body, and/or your state attorney general or office of consumer affairs, if appropriate. You should also write your local "Better Business Bureau," as well as any "Trade Association" that might be of some aid.

There are about 200 Better Business Bureaus ("BBBs") throughout America.

Better Business Bureaus

There are about 200 Better Business Bureaus ("BBBs") throughout America. These non-profit agencies not only provide general information on a wide variety of products and services, but also keep records on the background of local businesses, as well as their history for resolving complaints. Many BBBs will contact a business in an attempt to resolve your complaint, and you should always inquire if this can be done. The address and telephone number of your local BBB is in the telephone directory.

Trade Associations

Groups of businesses marketing similar products or services often form "trade associations" to promote their common goals. The primary objective of a trade association is to further the business of the association's members. Many associations have realized that policing their membership to weed out bad members and actively addressing consumer complaints will enhance the business of the overall membership. As a result, most trade associations not only will help consumers resolve problems with association members, but also will pressure their members to satisfy a disgruntled consumer's demands. Bar associations and the other private professional and contracting associations listed on pages 84-85 are all forms of trade associations.

If you cannot get relief from a business, ask whether it is a member of any trade association. If it is, address your concerns to the association. A list of some of the larger trade associations, compiled by the U.S. Office of Consumer Affairs, is set forth on pages 96-100.

Be A Squeaky Wheel

Whenever you complain about a business to a government agency, the BBB, a trade association, or other third party, always explain your problem and what you have done to get the matter resolved. Your complaint also should specify what relief you seek.

Unfortunately, government agencies, in particular, often are far less responsive than we expect them to be.

Unfortunately, government agencies, in particular, often are far less responsive than we expect them to be. The squeaky wheel gets the grease, however. Therefore, be a squeaky wheel and in a soft-spoken, civil tone, pester the government for action if none is forthcoming after a reasonable time. Those who zealously seek action are far more likely to get relief than those who fail to follow up on their complaints.

Attorney Demand Letters

If you cannot get satisfaction from a business directly, and neither the government, the BBB, nor any trade or professional association has remedied your problem, you should retain a lawyer to write a letter to the business, demanding relief on your behalf. While many businesses routinely ignore consumer correspondence, they will respond favorably to attorney demand letters, since the cost to remedy a consumer's complaint is often far less than the attorneys' fees needed to defend a consumer's lawsuit. Most attorneys charge only a small fee to write a demand letter.

While many businesses routinely ignore consumer correspondence, they will respond favorably to attorney demand letters.

Contingency Arrangements

If an attorney demand letter does not help, and the business is unwilling to negotiate with your attorney, ask your attorney whether he will sue the business for a "contingency fee." Under a contingency fee arrangement, the lawyer's fee is a percentage (usually one-third) of any amount he recovers for you. Thus, if the lawyer recovers $1000 for you, he will get $333 and you will get $666. If the lawyer is unable to recover any money for you, you will both get nothing.

The advantage of a contingency fee arrangement is that you will not have to pay your lawyer an hourly fee for his services, which could total thousands of dollars. Note, however, that in many contingency fee arrangements, the client is required to pay all "costs" of the lawsuit. Costs include filing and witness fees, copying or transcript charges, or any other expense incurred by the lawyer on your behalf, other than the lawyer's fee. Also note that in many states, the party losing a lawsuit may be required to pay the winning party's attorneys' fees, and these fees will be payable even if the losing party was represented on a contingency fee basis.

Unless your case against a business is a good one, the amount at stake is over $20,000, and the business is solvent, you probably will not find a lawyer willing to represent you on a contingency basis. You then have three alternatives: (1) hire counsel to prosecute your lawsuit for an hourly fee; (2) prosecute the lawsuit yourself without legal representation; or (3) give up. Ask your attorney whether it makes economic sense for you to hire him on an hourly basis. If he advises it does not, ask him whether he believes you can prosecute a lawsuit by yourself.

Small claims courts allow laymen to prosecute claims under a certain dollar value without lawyers.

Suing In Small Claims Court

Prosecuting lawsuits in most courts is beyond the ability of most consumers. Your lawyer is likely to advise that you are incapable of prosecuting an action in any court other than a "small claims" court. Small claims courts allow laymen to prosecute claims under a certain dollar value without lawyers. *In many small claims courts, both sides are not allowed to have a lawyer!*

The dollar value limit varies from state to state, and your lawyer can tell you whether your claim can be brought in a small claims court. If a small claims court is available, visit the court and ask if the court provides any written instructions and forms for prosecuting a lawsuit. If instructions are available, follow them to the letter.

Most actions in small claims court begin by the consumer paying a modest fee and filling out a "Complaint" form, which simply sets forth the parties' names and addresses, as well as the consumer's grievance. The complaining party is usually called the "Plaintiff" or "Petitioner." The other party usually is called the "Defendant" or "Respondent." The "Complaint" must specifically identify the Plaintiff's damages and any other relief he seeks.

At the time you fill out the Complaint, you also will have to fill out a "Summons" form, which will identify the names and addresses of each party and "command" the Defendant to appear in court to respond to your Complaint. After completing the Complaint and Summons forms, you usually give these forms to the court clerk who will assign your case a number and stamp that number on the forms. In most states, you are then required to have a licensed process server (look in the Yellow Pages under "Process Servers") deliver a copy of your Complaint and Summons to the Defendant.

After the process server delivers a copy of your Summons and Complaint to the Defendant, the Defendant usually has between 20 and 30 days to file an "Answer," which is simply a response to the allegations made in your Complaint. In most states, the Defendant is required to mail you a copy of his Answer. If no Answer is filed within the time allowed, you should ask the court clerk for a "default" form which, when filled out and filed with the court, asks the court to enter a verdict in your favor.

If an Answer is timely filed, most courts then require you to request the clerk of court to set a trial date. After the clerk sets your case for trial, some courts require you to notify the Defendant of the trial date.

Note that the Defendant may make a claim against you at the time he files his Answer. Such claims are called "Counterclaims," and in most instances, you are required to file a response (usually called a "Reply") to the Counterclaim within a specified period (usually 20 days). If you fail to file a Reply to a Counterclaim, the Defendant may file a default notice against you! Remember that you always file original papers with the court and mail copies to your opponent.

Trials

Most small claims courts set trials within two months of your request.

Most small claims courts set trials within two months of your request. You are responsible for gathering all evidence necessary to support your position. That means you must gather any witnesses you believe will testify on your behalf, as well as any documents that appear to prove your case. If a witness will not voluntarily appear, you can require him to appear with a "subpoena," which is a form issued by the court clerk commanding the witness to appear and give testimony. You may have to pay a fee for the subpoena to be issued, and in most courts, the subpoena has to be delivered to the witness by a licensed process server. Many courts also require you to pay the witness a nominal fee to appear.

If a witness or your opponent has documents you wish to introduce into evidence, you can obtain these documents by delivering a "subpoena duces tecum" to the witness or opponent. A "subpoena duces tecum" lists the documents you are requesting and requires the recipient to bring these documents to the trial. The subpoena duces tecum is obtained and delivered in the same manner as a regular subpoena.

Small claims trials often are very much like those featured on the popular television program, "The People's Court." After each party is sworn in, and the judge explains any applicable courtroom procedures, you will be given a chance to explain why you believe your Complaint should be granted. Be sure to show the judge all documentary evidence supporting your position. The judge is likely to ask you questions, and he will allow your opponent to question you as well. You then should have any witnesses supporting your story testify. Both the judge and your opponent also may question them.

Small claims trials often are very much like those featured on the popular television program, "The People's Court."

After you have presented all evidence supporting your position, your opponent will have an opportunity to explain his position and present any documents or witnesses he believes support that position. You and the judge will have a chance to question your opponent and any witnesses that testify for him. If you believe your opponent or any witness has lied, ask questions that will expose the lies.

After each side has finished introducing evidence, and both the parties and all witnesses have been fully questioned, the judge will either render a decision immediately or decide the case later, notifying each party by mail. The judge's decision is called a "judgment," and usually will require the losing party to pay the winning party a sum of money. Just because you have obtained a judgment does not mean you will get paid, however. Some courts allow the losing party to appeal the court's decision, and even in situations where no appeals are taken or allowed, many losing parties refuse to pay judgments entered against them. If the Defendant refuses to pay, ask the court clerk (or a lawyer) what methods are available to "enforce" the judgment (that is, make the Defendant pay). The methods available for enforcing judgments are too varied and complicated to explain within the space limitations of this book, but you can ask for help from a local attorney. In fact, we recommend that you consult with a lawyer about collecting judgments or any aspect of filing suit.

CONCLUSION

If you have read this far, you have earned your "Ph.D." in purchasing savvy! Put into practice what you have read, and there will be few problems for which you will not be prepared. If you nevertheless run into problems with a business you cannot resolve on your own, do not hesitate to contact a qualified lawyer for advice. Early intervention by counsel on your behalf can often resolve seemingly minor disputes that might otherwise turn into major problems.

Good Luck!

Trade Associations

(Source: U.S. Office of Consumer Affairs)

Ms. Ann Lawrence, Director
Education and Conventions
**American Apparel
Manufacturers Association**
2500 Wilson Boulevard
Suite 301
Arlington, VA 22201
(703) 524-1864
Membership: Manufacturers of
clothing.

Mr. John W. Johnson, Executive Vice
President
American Collectors Association
4040 West 70th Street
P.O. Box 39106
Minneapolis, MN 55439-0106
(612) 926-6547
Membership: Collection services han-
dling overdue accounts for retail, profes-
sional and commercial credit grantors.

Ms. Jane Marden, Director
Consumer Affairs
Ms. Linda Wood, Associate Director
Community Affairs
American Gas Association
1515 Wilson Boulevard
Arlington, VA 22209
(703) 841-8583
Membership: Distributors and trans-
porters of natural gas.

American Health Care Association
1201 L Street, N.W.
Washington, DC 20005-4014
(202) 842-4444
(800) 321-0343
(toll free-publications only)
Membership: State associations of
long-term health care facilities.

**American Hotel and Motel
Association**
1201 New York Avenue, N.W.
Suite 600
Washington, DC 20005-3931
(written inquires only)

Membership: State and regional
hotel associations.

**American Newspaper Publishers
Assn. Credit Bureau Inc.**
P.O. Box 17022
Dulles International Airport
Washington, DC 20041
(703) 648-1038
Investigates fraudulent advertising
published in newspapers.

**American Orthotic and
Prosthetic Association**
1650 King Street, Suite 500
Alexandria, VA 22314-1885
(703) 836-7116
Represents member companies that
custom fit or manufacture components
for patients with prostheses or orthoses.

Mr. James A. Morrissey, Director
Communications Division
**American Textile Manufacturers
Institute**
1801 K Street, N.W.
Suite 900
Washington, DC 20006
(202) 862-0552
Membership: Textile mills which pro-
duce a variety of textile products, e.g.
clothing, using natural and man-
made fibers.

Better Hearing Institute
P.O. Box 1840
Washington, DC 20013
(703) 642-0580
(800) EAR-WELL (toll free)
Membership: Professionals and other
who help persons with impaired
hearing. Provides voluntary mediation between consumers and hearing
aid dispensers.

Consumer Affairs
Blue Cross and Blue Shield Association
Metro Square-Phase II
655 15th Street, N.W.
Suite 350F
Washington, DC 20005
(202) 626-4780
Membership: Local Blue Cross and Blue Shield plans in the United States, Canada and Jamaica.

Ms. Caroline C. Ortado
Administrator, Consumer Protection Bureau
Boat Owners Association of the United States (BOAT/U.S.)
880 South Pickett Street
Alexandria, VA 22304-0730
(703) 823-9550
Consumer protection bureau serves as a mediator in disputes between boat owners and the marine industry. BOAT/U.S. also works closely with the U.S. Coast Guard to monitor safety defect problems.

Mr. Richard N. "Ned" Hopper
Director of Governmental Affairs
Carpet and Rug Institute
1155 Connecticut Avenue, N.W.
Suite 500
Washington, DC 20036
(written inquires only)
Membership: Manufacturers of carpets, rugs, bath mats and bedspreads; suppliers of raw materials and services to the industry.

Mr. Robert M. Fells, Assistant Secretary
Cemetery Consumer Service Counsel
P.O. Box 3574
Washington, DC 20007
(703) 379-6426
Industry-sponsored dispute resolution program. Other consumer information about cemetery practices and rules available on request.

Children's Advertising Review Unit (CARU)
Counsel of Better Business Bureaus, Inc.
845 Third Avenue
New York, NY 10022
(212) 754-1354
Handles consumer complaints about fraudulent and deceptive advertising related to children.

Ms. Lorra Christie, Director
Ethics and Consumer Affairs
Direct Marketing Association (DMA)
6 East 43rd Street
New York, NY 10017-4646
(written complaints only)
Membership: Members who market goods and services directly to consumers using direct mail, catalogs, telemarketing, magazine and newspaper ads, and broadcast advertising.

DMA operates the Mail Order Action Line, Mail Preference Service and Telephone Preference Service.

For problems with a mail order company, write:
Mail Order Action Line
6 East 43rd Street
New York, NY 10017

To remove your name from a direct mail list, write:
Mail Preference Service
P.O. Box 3861
Grand Central Station
New York, NY 10163

To remove your name from a telephone solicitation list, write:
Telephone Preference Service
6 East 43rd Street
New York, NY 10017

Mr. William Rogal
Code Administrator
Direct Selling Association
1776 K Street, N.W. , Suite 600
Washington, DC 20006-2387
(202) 293-5760
Membership: Manufacturers and distributors selling consumer products door-to-door and through home-party plans.

Ms. Sally Browne, Executive
Director Consumer Affairs
Electronic Industries Association
2001 Pennsylvania Avenue, N.W. ,
10th Floor
Washington, DC 20006
(202) 457-4977
Complaint assistance program, consumer education, etc. concerning televisions, video cassette recorders and other video systems, audio products, personal computers and communication electronic products.

**Funeral Service Consumer
Arbitration Program (FSCAP)**
1614 Central Street
Evanston, IL 60201
(800) 662-7666 (toll free)
Third-party dispute resolution program sponsored by the National Funeral Directors Association.

Ms. Carole M. Rogin, President
Market Development
Hearing Industries Association
1255 23rd Street, N.W.
Washington, DC 20037-1174
(202) 833-1411
Membership: Companies engaged in the manufacture and/or sale of electronic hearing aids, their components, parts and related products and services on a national basis.

**Home Owners Warranty
Corporation (HOW) Operation
Center**
P.O. Box 152087
Irving, TX 75015-2087
(800) 433-7657 (toll free)
Third-party dispute resolution program for new homes built by HOW-member home builders.

Ms. Jill A. Wolper, Manager
Consumer Affairs and Education
Insurance Information Institute
110 William Street
New York, NY 10038
(800) 942-4242 (toll free)
National Insurance Consumer Helpline is a resource for consumers with automobile and home insurance questions. The Helpline is open Monday through Friday from 8 am to 8 pm.

**Major Appliance Consumer
Action Panel (MACAP)**
20 North Wacker Drive
Chicago, IL 60606
(312) 984-5858
(800) 621-0477 (toll free)
Third-party dispute resolution program of the major appliance industry.

Mr. John E. Dianis
Executive Vice President
**Monument Builders of North
America**
1740 Ridge Avenue
Evanston, IL 60201
(708) 869-2031
Membership: Cemetery monument retailers, manufacturers and wholesalers; bronze manufacturers and suppliers. Consumer brochures available on request.

National Advertising Division (NAD)

A Division of the Counsel of Better Business Bureaus, Inc.
845 Third Avenue
New York, NY 10022
(212) 754-1320
Program: Handles consumer complaints about the truth and accuracy of national advertising.

National Association of Personnel Consultants

3133 Mt. Vernon Avenue
Alexandria, VA 22305
(703) 684-0180
Membership: Private employment agencies.

Accrediting Commission
National Association of Trade and Technical Schools

2251 Wisconsin Avenue, N.W.
Washington, DC 20007-4181
(202) 333-1021
(written inquiries only)
Membership: Private schools providing job training.

Accrediting Commission
National Food Processors Association

1401 New York Avenue, N.W.
Washington, DC 20005
(202) 639-5939
Membership: Commercial packers of such food products as fruit, vegetables, meat, poultry, seafood, and canned, frozen, dehydrated, pickled and other preserved food items.

Ms. Cindy Donahue
Assistant To Executive Director
National Home Study Counsel

1601 18th Street, N.W.
Washington, DC 20009
(written inquires only)
Membership: Home study (correspondence) schools.

National Tire Dealers and Retreaders Association

1250 Eye Street, N.W.
Suite 400
Washington, DC 20005
(202) 789-2300
(800) 876-8372 (toll free)
Membership: Independent tire dealers and retreaders.

Department of Consumer Affairs
National Turkey Federation

11319 Sunset Hills Road
Reston, VA 22090-5205
(written inquiries only)
Membership: Turkey growers, turkey hatcheries, turkey breeders, processors, marketers, and allied industry firms and poultry distributors.

Mr. Craig Halverson
Assistant Executive Director
Photo Marketing Association

3000 Picture Place
Jackson, MI 49201
(written complaints only)
Membership: Retailers of photo equipment, film and supplies; firms developing and printing film.

Mrs. Jane Meyer
Director of Consumer Affairs
The Soap and Detergent Association

475 Park Avenue South
New York, NY 10016
(212) 725-1262
Membership: Manufacturers of soap, detergents, fatty acids and glycerine; raw material suppliers.

Tele-Consumer Hotline

1910 K Street, N.W., Suite 610
Washington, DC 20006
(202) 223-4371 (voice/TDD)
Provides information on special telephone products and services for persons with disabilities, selecting a long distance company, money saving tips for people on low income, reducing unsolicited phone calls, telemarketing fraud, dealing with the phone

company and other issues. All telephone assistance and publications are free of charge, and Spanish-speaking counselors are available.

Ms. Diane Cardinale
Assistant Communications Director
Toy Manufacturers of America
200 Fifth Avenue, Room 740
New York, NY 10010
(212) 675-1141
Membership: American toy manufacturers.

Mr. Robert E. Whitley, President
U.S. Tour Operators Associations (USTOA)
211 East 51st Street
Suite 12-B
New York, NY 10022
(212) 944-5727
Membership: Wholesale tour operators, common carriers, suppliers and providers of travel services.

Index